Construction Paper Poems

MT Stolte

Construction Paper Poems by MT (Matthew Thomas) Stolte

ISBN: 978-1-7353850-1-3

First Edition

eMTeVisPub

http://www.lulu.com/spotlight/emtevispub

This book was made possible in part by a generous grant from Dane Arts.

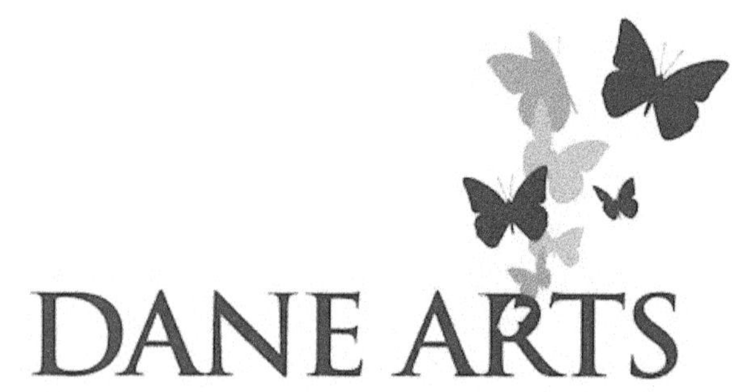

for Sherryl Kay Stolte

Introduction to *Construction Paper Poems*

In 2010 I decided to use a local print shop (Lakeside Printing Cooperative) to publish the 1st of 4 chapbooks in the style of the avant poetry magazines *Score* & *Xerolage* (card stock cover, 8.5 x 11", side stapled). Indeed, mIEKAL aND was still using this shop for *Xerolage* until shortly thereafter he switched to exclusively online printers (the shop itself closed by January 2019, competing with digital media). Of my 4 projects, I felt that this was the most successful in terms of its bulky, solid black imagery on white. Likewise titled *Construction Paper Poems*, it was my 4th print project of the year, eMTeVisPub #4.

COVID-19 hit Wisconsin mid-March, 2020. I lost my job (discharged, no misconduct) & focused on print projects. In the midst of several projects ready to print, I reopened the *CPP* ms & decided to make more works, to give me art making time instead of solely art publishing time.

Like the earlier works, most of the new poems were made with black construction paper on white card stock. What with a year of working with unemployment, I received with every mailing a two-sided sheet in 21 languages titled "Unemployment Insurance Interpreter and Translation Services". I saved & cut the sheets into thirds to work on, a convenient size for sending out as mail art as well. Some of these works were sent out before publication.

Many of the works are essentially glyphs, the form created by sketching with crayons. Some come easy, some do not. Other works are collages of simple letter forms, often Ks & Ds representing figures, & doors or moons. Making new works in 2020, some of the compositions became more abstract, using the cuttings from letter forms without preconceived ideas of what I was creating. Some concrete dollars & cents poems appear throughout (see *Concrete Dollars and Cents Poems* 2nd edition, by the author, published in 2020 by eMTeVisPub). BLM, acronym for Black Lives Matter, appears in some of the works as the movement gained popularity after the murder of George Floyd, May 25th, 2020.

construction
PAPER
POEMS
M.Stolte

Original cover of the eMTeVisPub chapbook, 2010

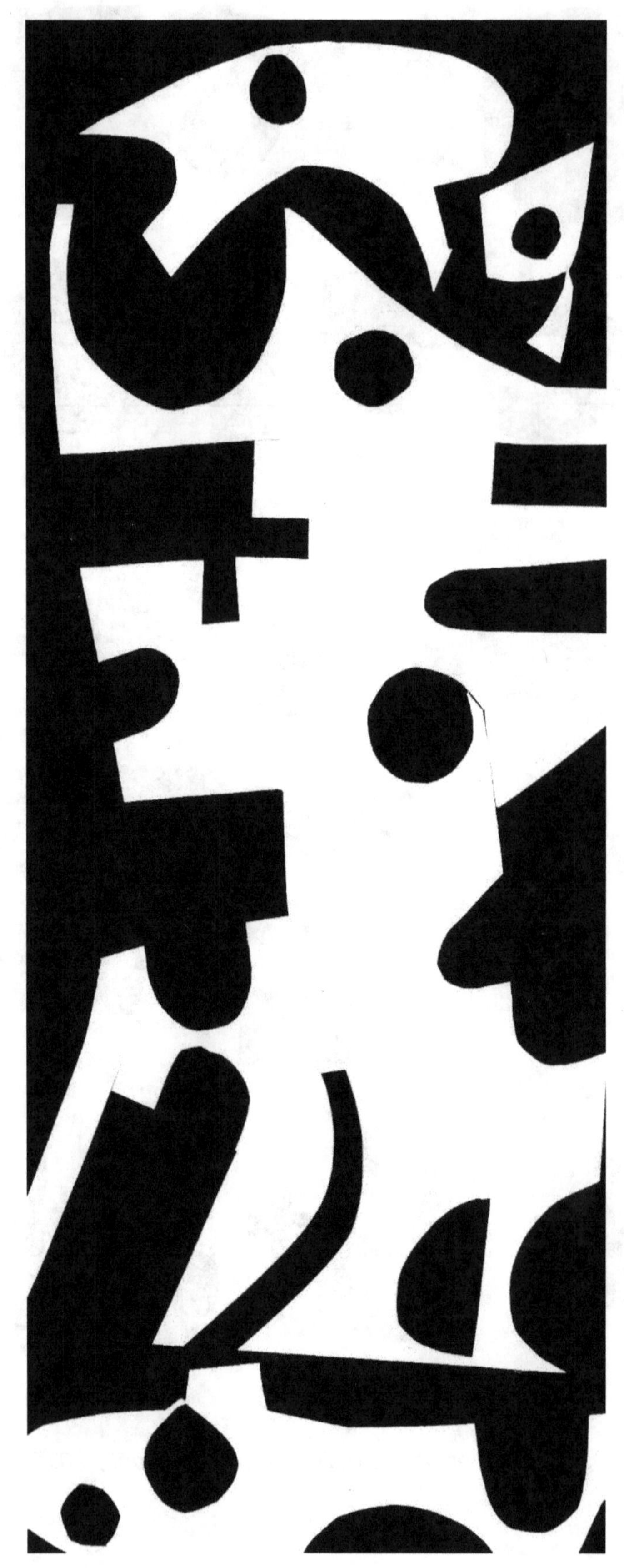

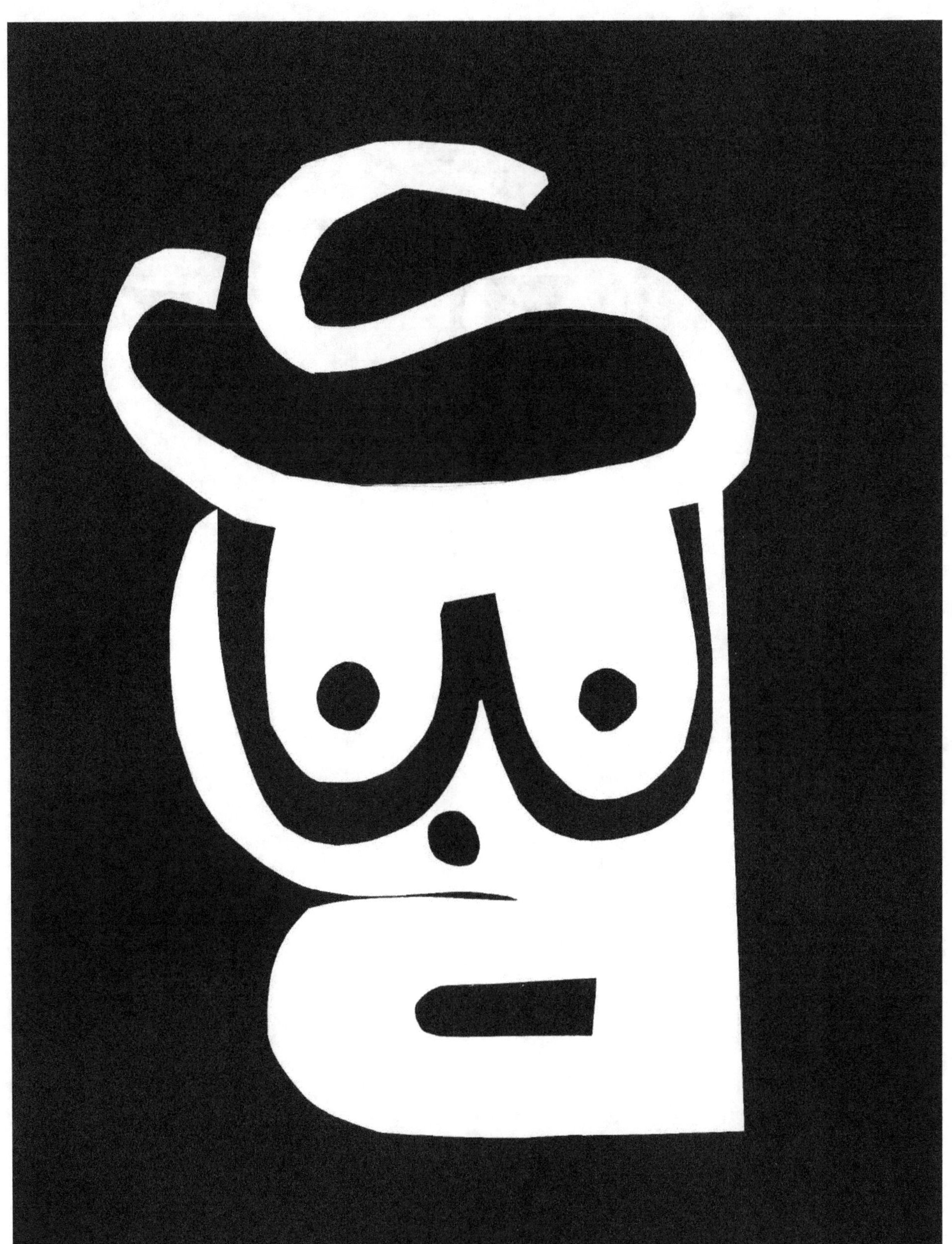

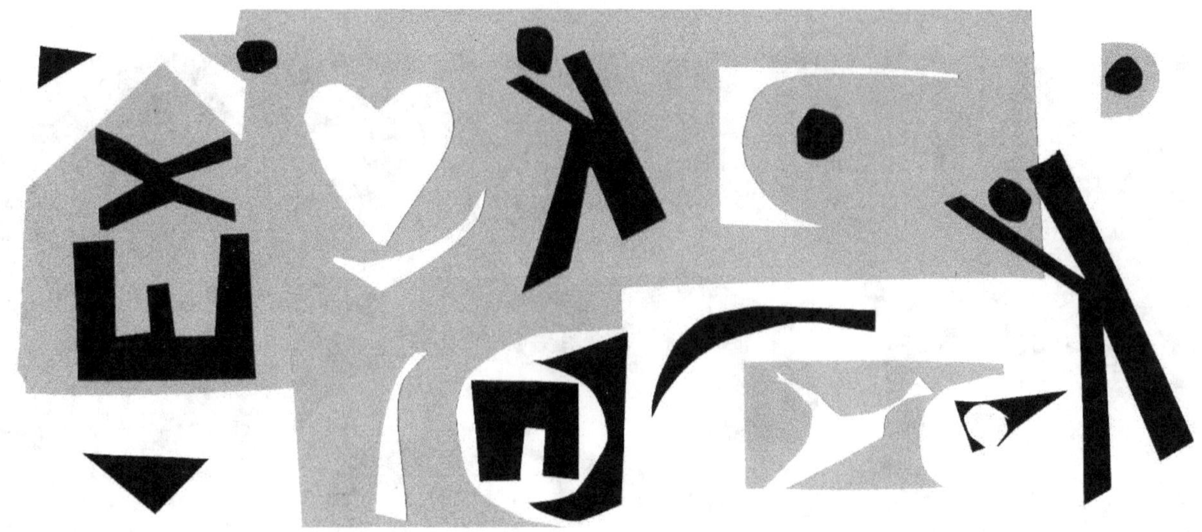

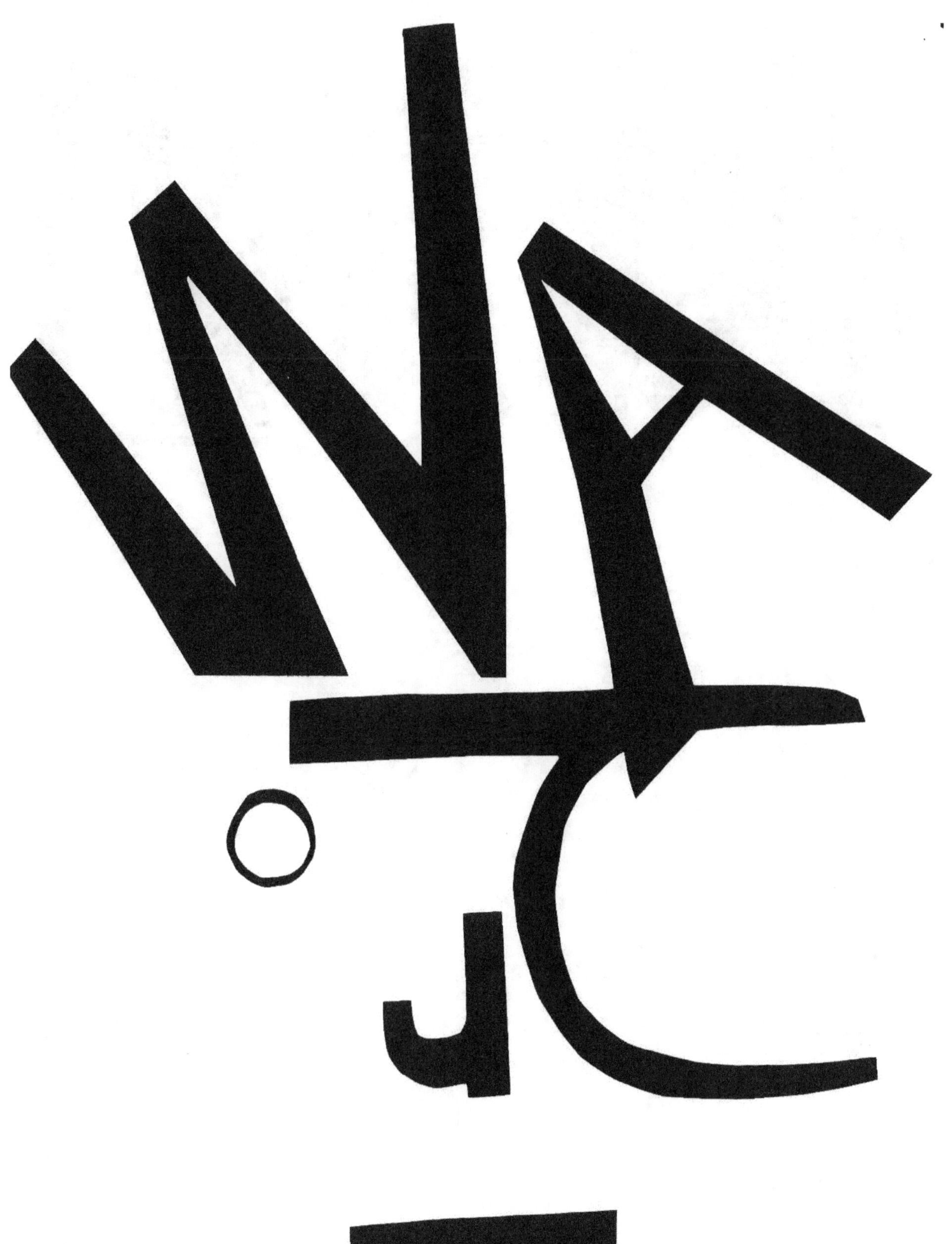

重要です！ 書には、あな の 益に関する権利、責任および／または失業手当につい を含み
の情報は かりと理解 よう してくださ 。ご あるいは 書類の翻訳をご 方は、営業
間中 414)435-7069 までお電話く い。通訳のサー スは無料で けら ます。

어 (rean)

중 안내! 이 리와 책임 및 급여에 관한 중요한 정보가 있습 이해하는
결정적으 번역된 실업보험 신청서가 필요하다면, 업무 이내어
435-7 도움을 무료로 받 수 다.

ภ ทย (Thai

คัญ! เอก หน้าที่ความรั และ ประ ท่านจำ ข้อมูลนี้
ห คำถามหรื 14) 435-7069 หาล่าม การโดย

Češt a (Czech)

D LEŽITÉ! Tento důležité informace ch p nezaměstnan odp osti a/aneb
ách. Je důležité a infor zuměli. e-li klá anebo necha eloži menty o
nezaměstnanosti, zavolejte na (414) 5-7069 v pracov bě. Tlu m bude pos nut bez e.

gracieusement par un interprète.

ຄົນລາວ (Laotian)

ສຳ... ສານນີ້ປະກອບມີຂໍ້ມູນສຳ... ກ່ຽວກັ... ຊອບ ແລະ/ຫຼື ເງິນຊ່ວຍເຫຼືອການຫວ່າງງານຂອງທ່າ...
...ວ່າທ່ານຕ້ອງເຂົ້າໃຈຂໍ້... ນີ້. ເພື່ອ... ແປເອກະສານ...
... ໃນລະຫວ່າງຊົ່ວ... ເຣັດວຽກ.

YOU

WISH

...ROT... Tài liệu này có... ặc quyền lợi thấ...
...n. B... hỏi... u về thông tin này... câu hỏi... ược dịch, xin g...
...trong... giờ làm việc. Chúng tôi sẽ... thông dịch viê...

ALTER

...话 Can... Mandar... Taiwanese)

...有关您的...利，责任和/... 重要信息。了解这... 要。如果要... 业文
...时间致电 (414)...069。... 提供翻译。

TO

TO PLEASE DO

Unemployment Insurance
...rpreter and Translatio... rvices

HEY YOU FEE

The di... ons b... -native Eng... eed t... one of the following languages.

IM...ORTA... his document contai... porta... unem... nt rights, respo... ities and/or ...
... It is critical that you understa... his in... o... or... nemploym... t documents
...ed, call (414) 435-7069 during... sines... An in... will... e pr... no cost... yo...

YOU

Spanis...

¡IMPORTANTE!... umento... ne in... ción importante so... su d... mp... su...
...neficios. E... ve q... ed entienda esta... ormaci... pre... ntas... qu...
...acionad... el d... pleo, llame al (4...) 435-7... ar... a. Le
proporcionaremos un intérprete s... ún c... ara usted.

MAIL ANY WAY

...mong)

...Dain... n tseem ceeb... muaj cai, cov... v lees r... iab/los
...b nta... ws tse... j yuav tsum nka...
...kev t... ov nt... ob hauj lwm uas txh...
rau (414) 435-7069 nyob rau lub sij hawm ua hauj lwm. Y... eeg txhais lus rau koj pub dawb.

Bosanski/Hrvats... /S... (B... /Cr... ian/Serbian)

VAŽNO! Ovaj d... PPEARING ...žne i... o Vašim pravima... ovom... ha i / ili... a za
...a razumet... RPLE ...e. Da bi... sta... pitanja ili pre... dol... ente o neza... osti, n...
...9 tokom radnog vremena. Prevodila... e vam... obezbeđe... spl...

Shqip (Albanian)

...ENDËSISHËM! ... përmban informacio... ndësish... dhje me të... punësisë,
...rgjegj... ë dhe / ... criticalshtë kritike q... ptoni k... acion. P... se të kemi
...mente... nyera, te... fononi (414) 435... 9 gjat... unës. ... ofrohet pa
kosto.

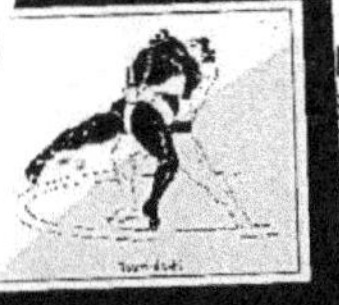

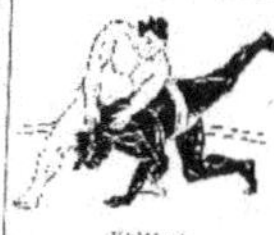

...ssian)

...данный документ содержит важную информацию о в... х прав... на трудоустройство, обязанностях
...отах. Важно, чтобы вы поня... ормацию. Если у... есть во...
...документов по безработице... номеру (414) 4... рабо...
...редоставля...

ANYTHING

Français (French)

IMPORTANT! Ce do... de... um f... imp... vos droits, ...ponsabilités et / ou avantages liés
au chômage. Il est e... c... e information. Pour poser d... questions ou faire traduire les
documents de chômage, appelez le (414) 435-7069 pendant les heures ouvrables. Vous pourrez être aidé

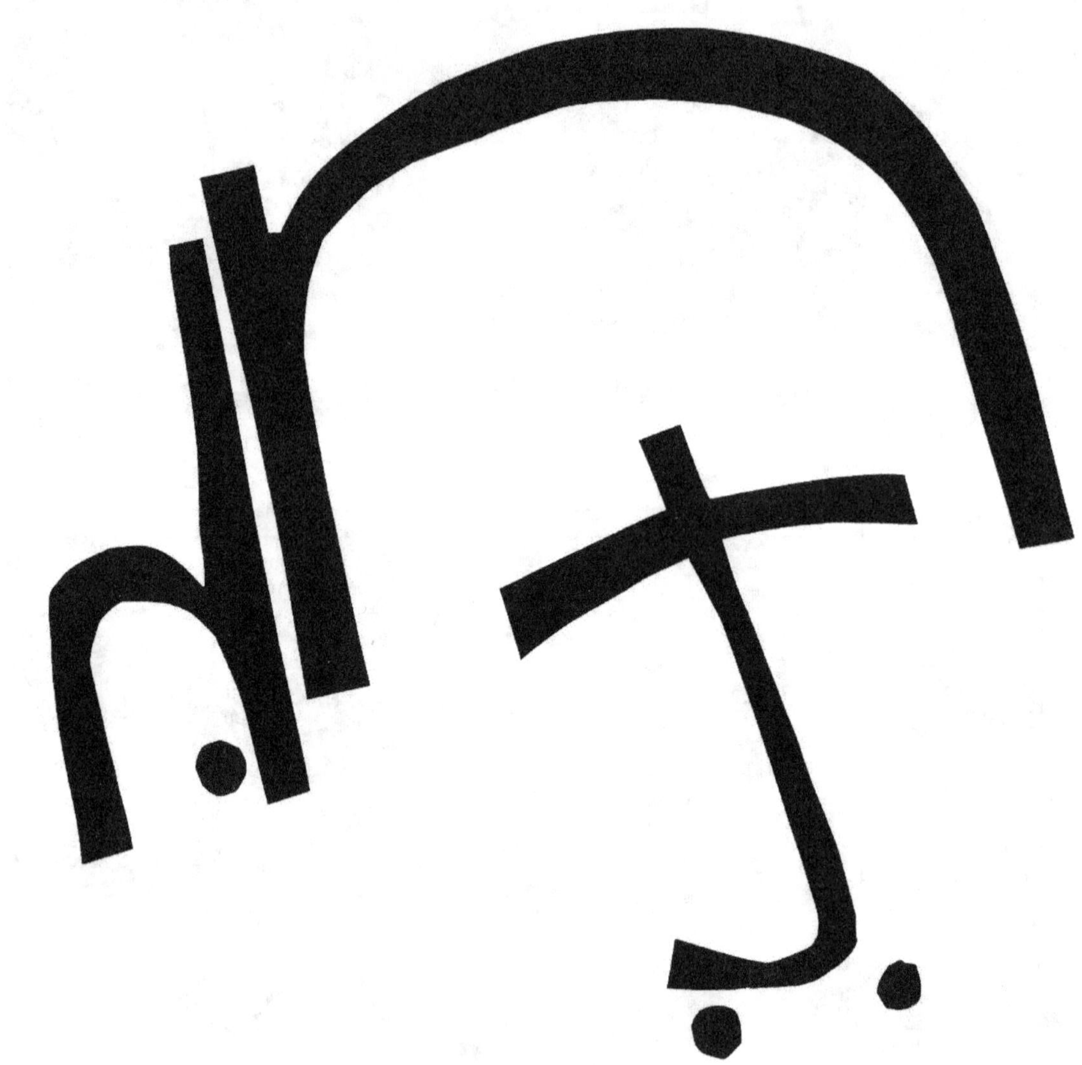

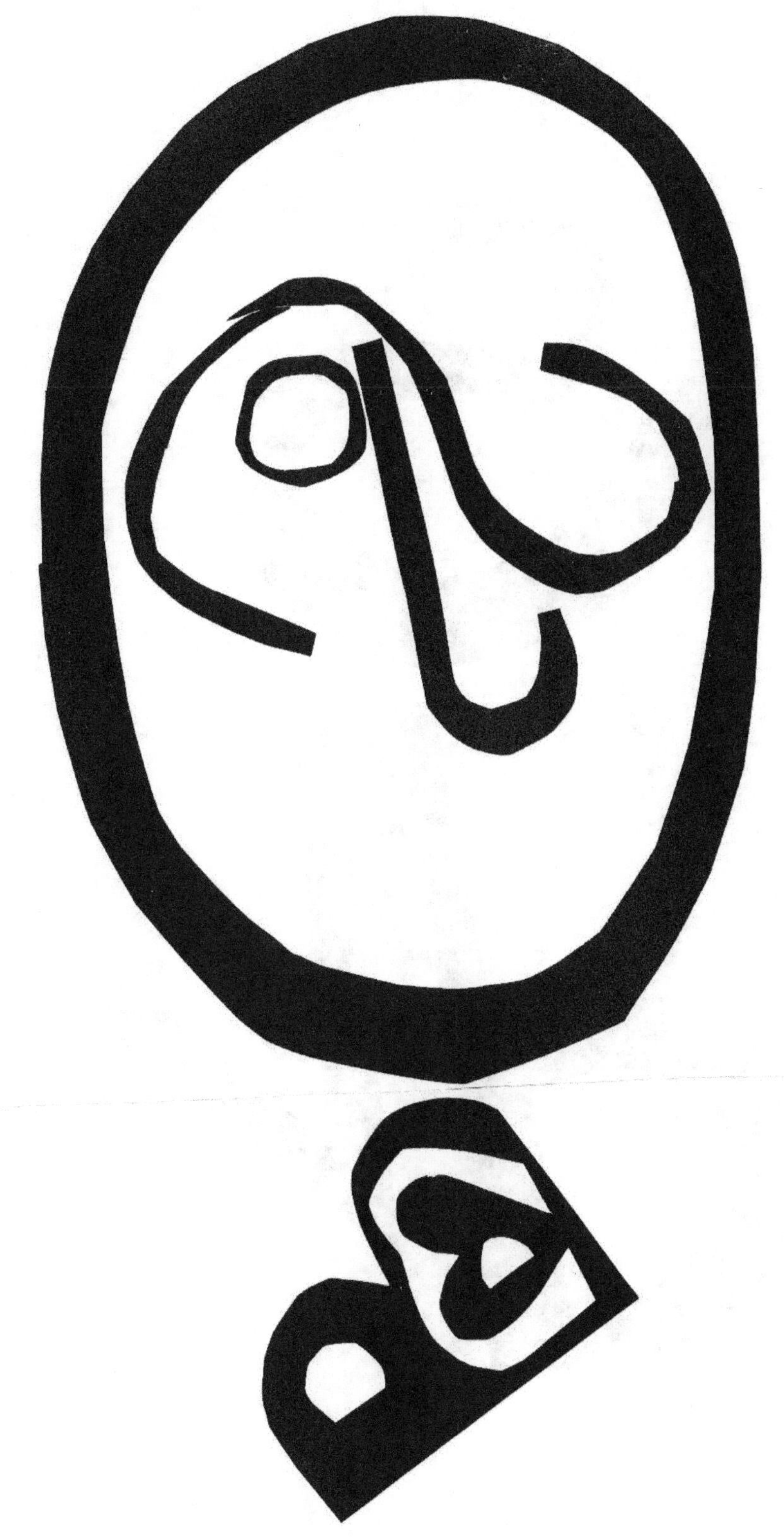

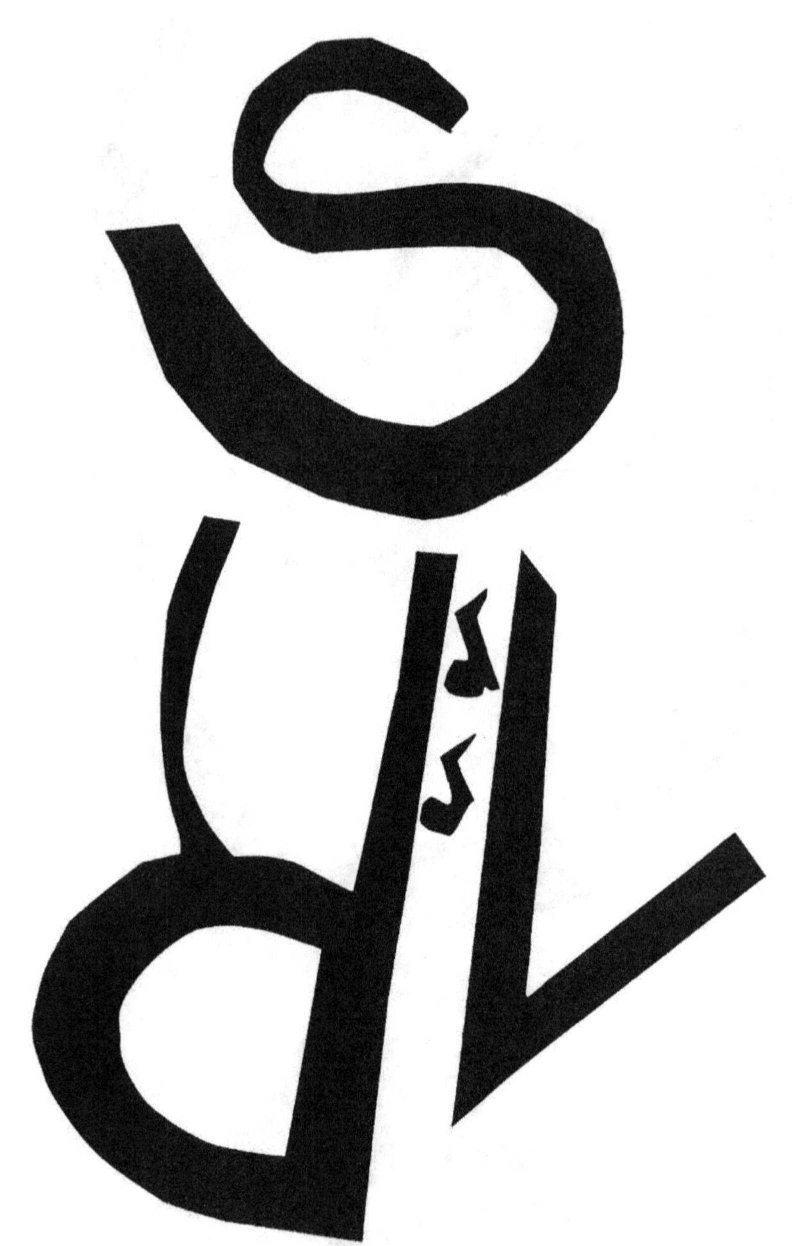

$PACE

$oil

$NOW

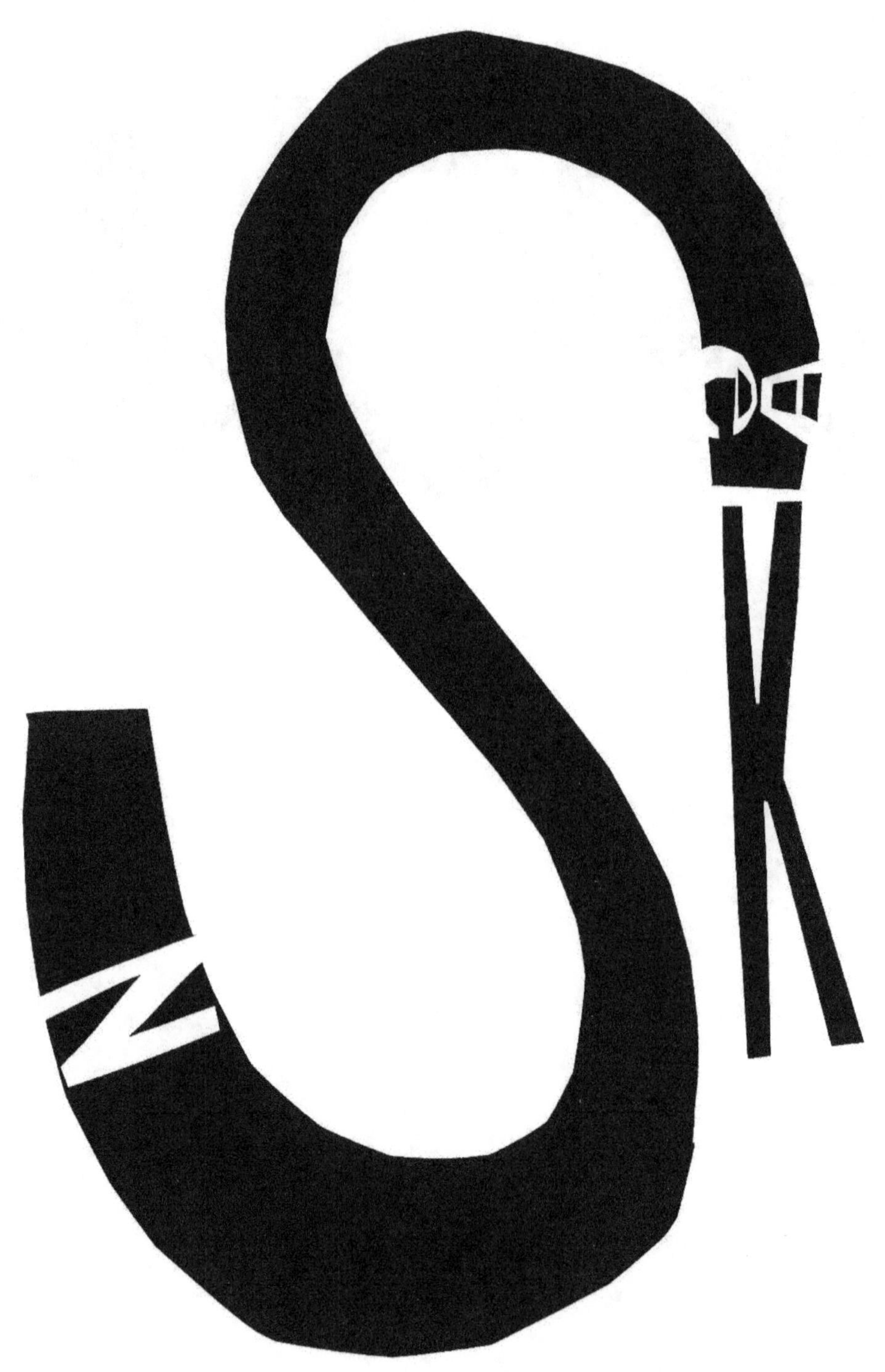

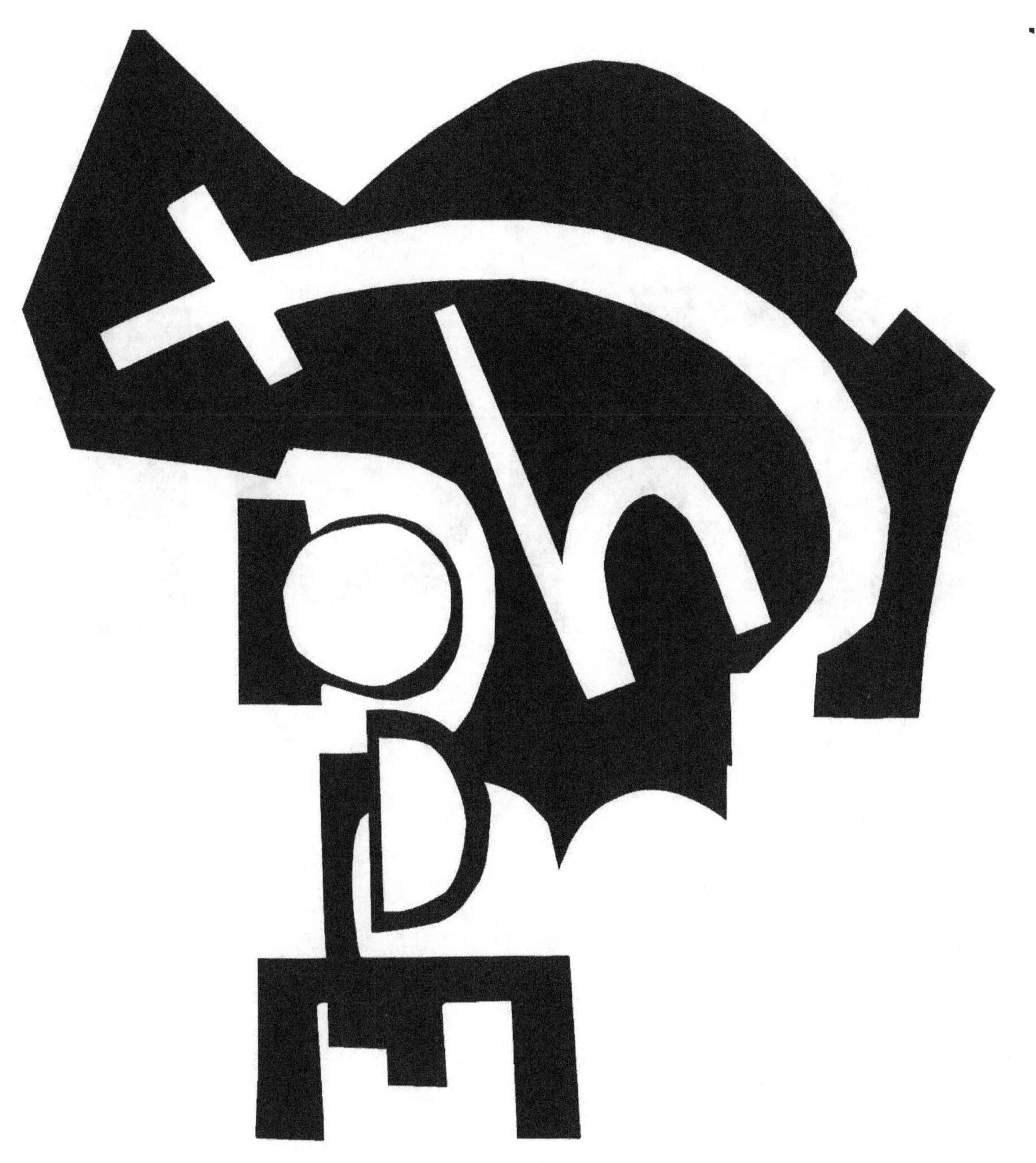

$HOE

$EA
$oil

$EA

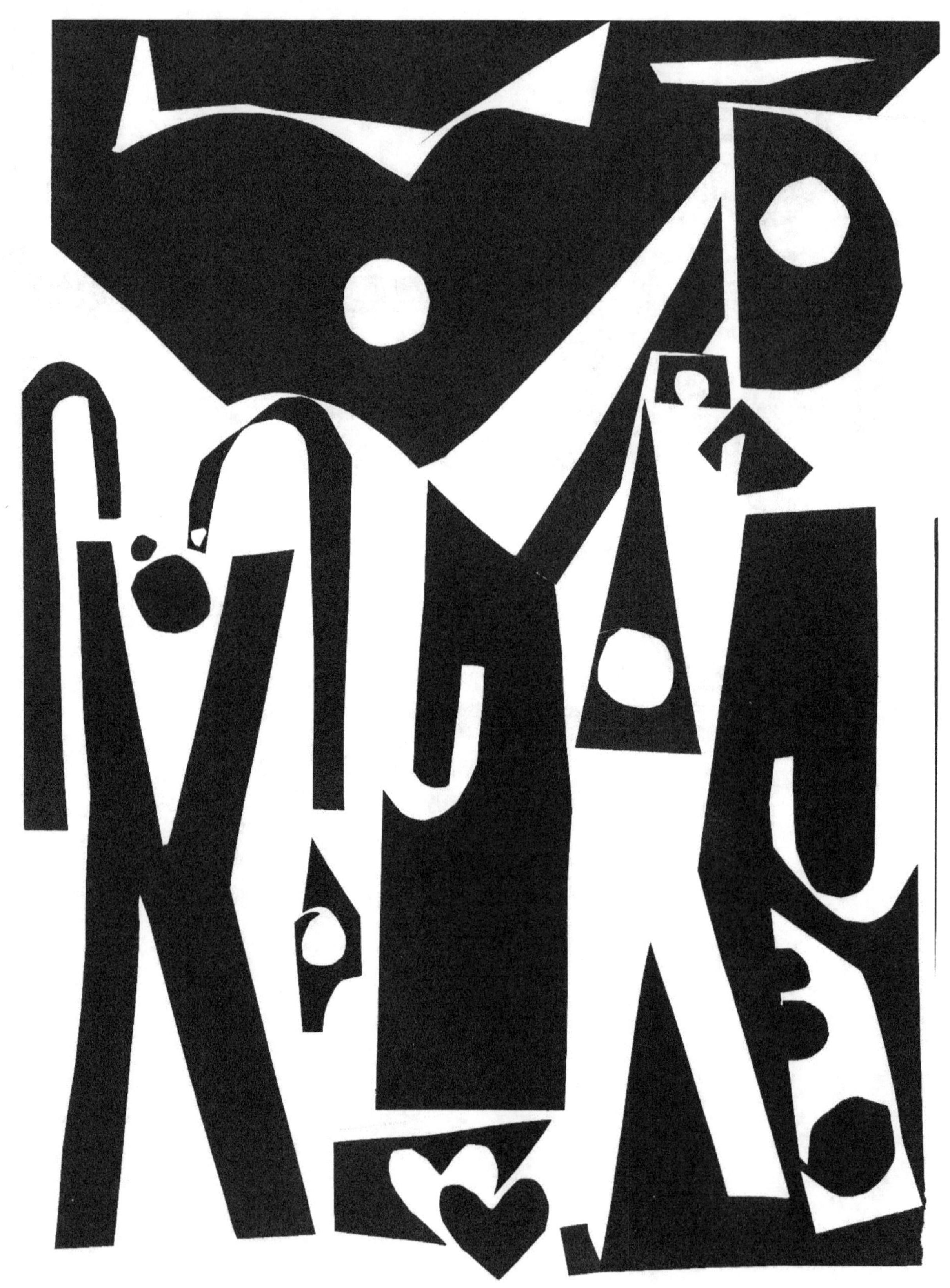

So aali (S ...)

HIIM AH! Dukumintigaan waxaa ku jira r ad muhiim ah absan xuquuqda
waajibaa a iyo / ama waxtarka. W daruu har uluu. aadkaan. Si aad u weydi gu
tarjumo kum iyada shaqo la' ta, wac -706 gu guda jiro saacadaha shaqa
lagu s bon digo aan l ash kuug .n.

Język i (P n)

W en ment a waż macje na tem acownika, jego ob zków i/
powiedzialn Wa pyś zroz informację. W celu informacji lub maczenie dokumentów
związanych z oń pod nr -7069 podczas godziny pra darmo z

हिन्दी (Hindi)

महत्वपूर्ण! इस के बेरोजगा धिकारों, जिम यों और / या ला नकारी
नि ह आ श्य आप इस जानकारी को समझें। ई प्रश्न पूछने या बेरो अनुवाद के
लिए, 435 पर का के दौरान करें। आपको मुफ्त में एक दु प्रद ।

عربي (Arabic)

هذه الوثيقة على معلومات مهمة حول حقوقك في البطالة ومسؤولياتك والمزايا التي تحصل عليها. من المهم أن تتفهم هذه المعلومات. لطرح أسئلة أو

So (Somali)

HIIM AH! Dukumintigaan waxaa ku jira mac o bs x daada shaq nta,
waajibaadka iyo / ama w arka. daruuri i aa n. weydiiso su'aal lagu
tarjumo dukument a o la a, wac (41 uda o s adaha . Turj ayaa
la siin doona o aan ash kuugu f

Język polski (Po

W E! Ten do t a ważne informa cownika, je po i/lub
o dzialnos zrozumiał tę in ormacji lub a maczenie d kument
zw h z pr nr (414) 435- zas godziny pracy. Sk ię za tłumaczen

हिन्दी (Hindi)

महत्व इस दस्त पके ब संबंधी अधिक जिम्मेदारियों औ लाभों के ब महत्वपूर्ण कारी
निहित है। यह ते कि आप नकारी को कोई प्र या बेरोजगा विजों के द के
, (414) 435-70 -समय के दौरान । मुफ्त में एक दुभाषिया प्रदा जाएगा

عربي (Arabic)

هذه الوثيقة على معلومات مهمة حول حقوقك في البطالة ومسؤولياتك والمزايا التي تحصل عليها. من المهم أن تتفهم هذه المعلومات. لطرح أسئلة أو

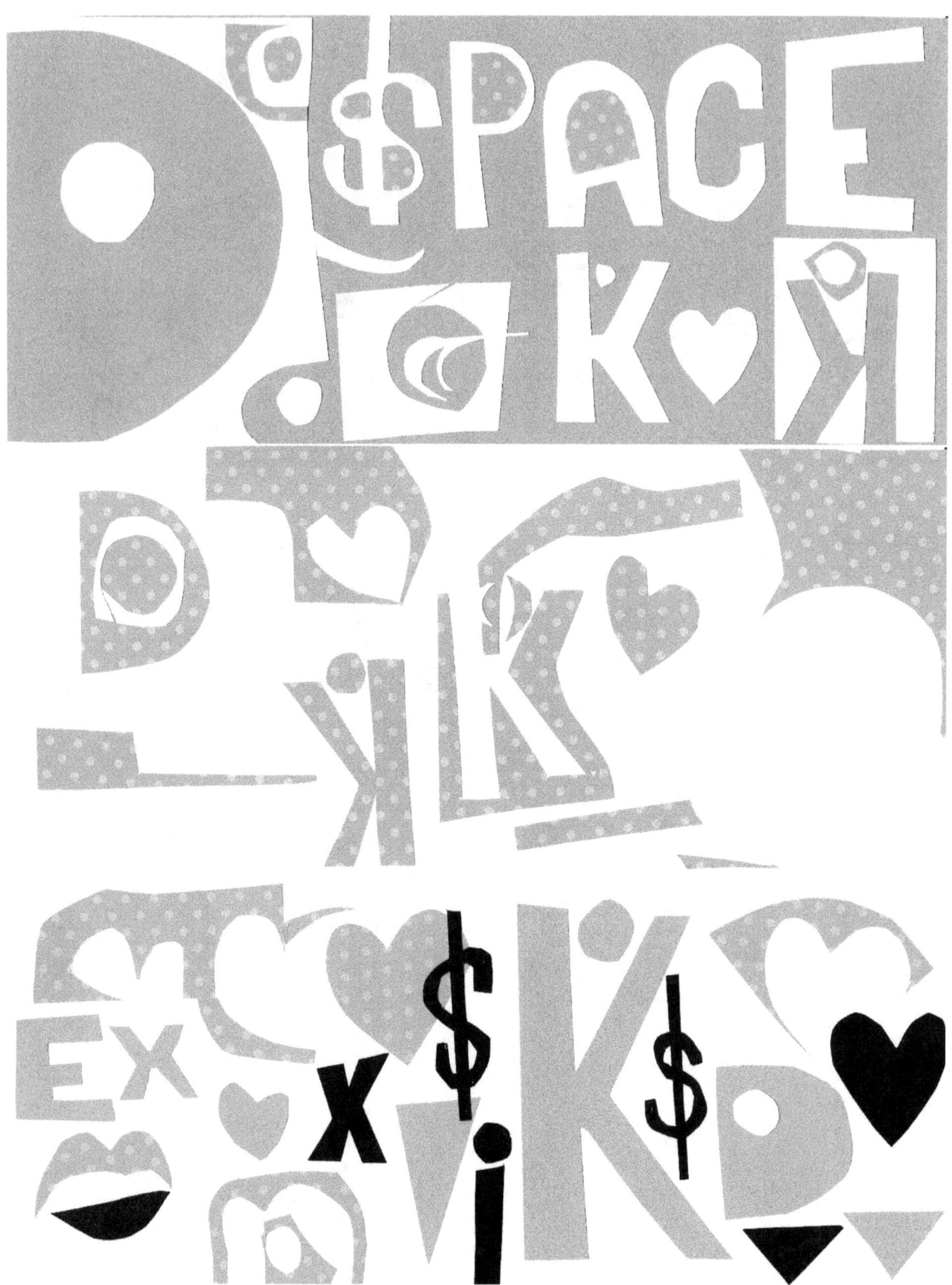
$PACE
EX

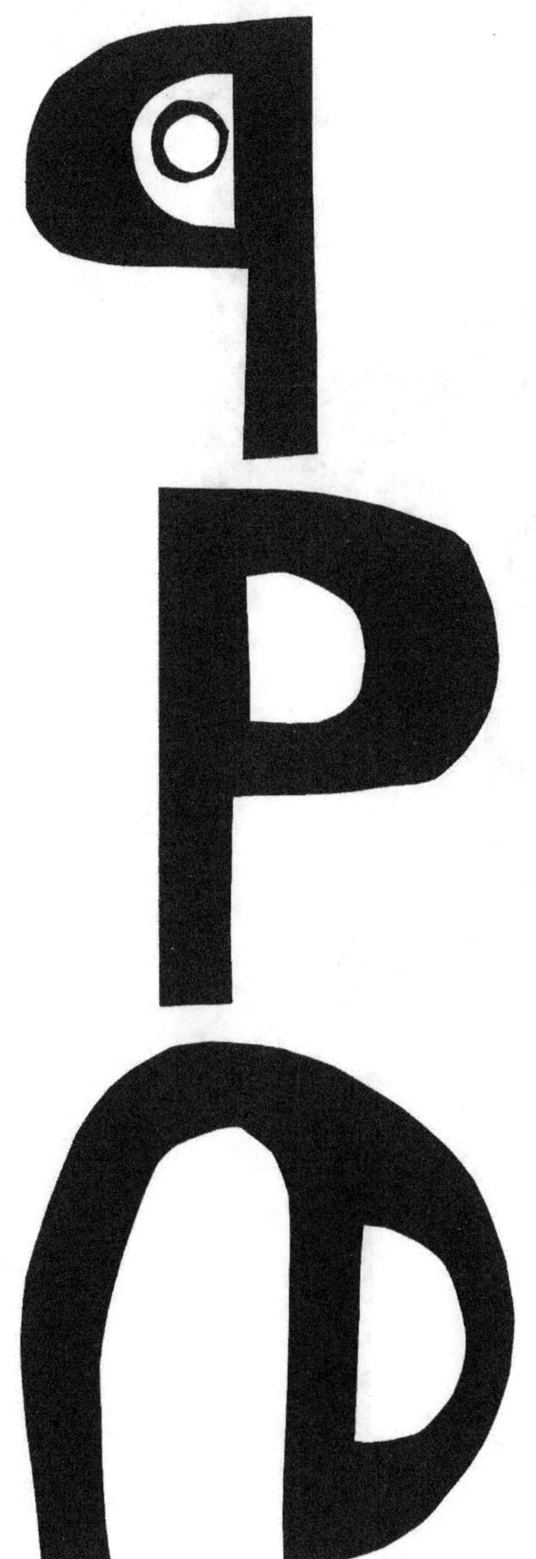

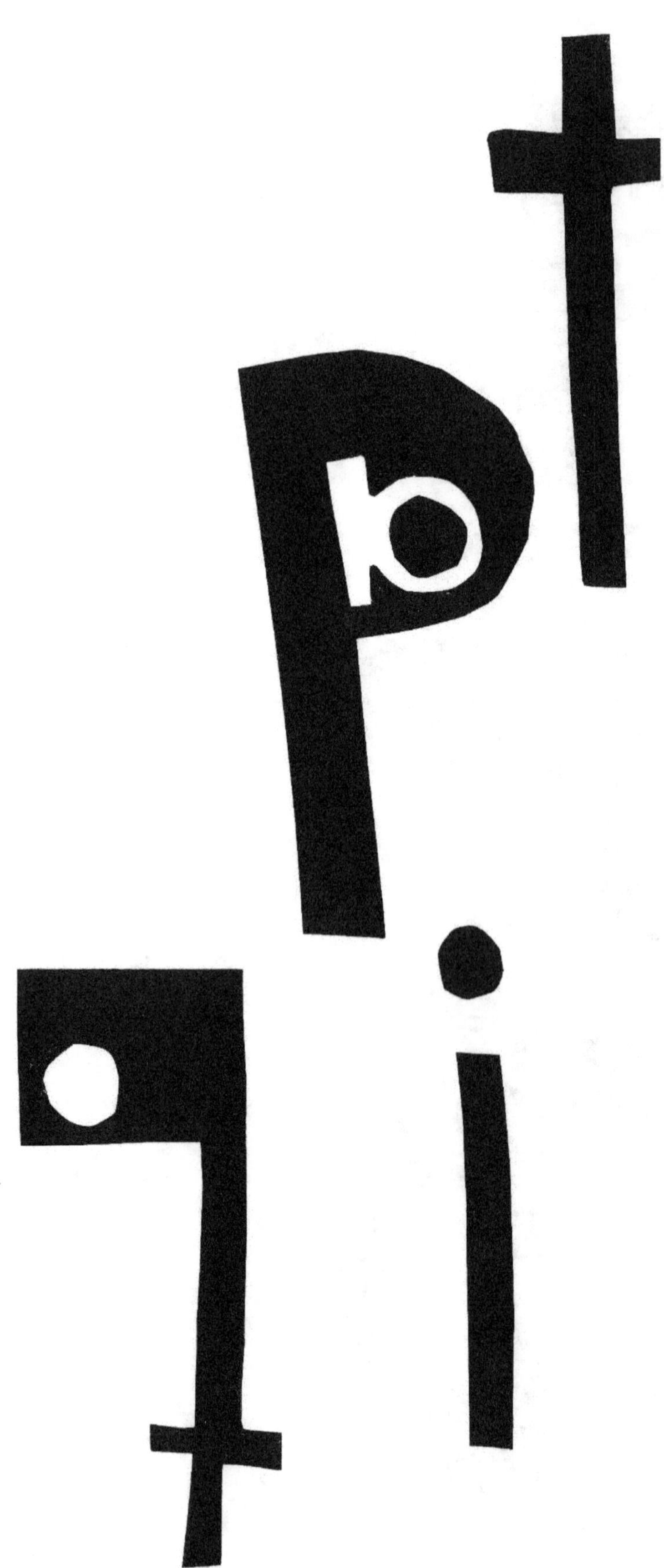

live
BLM

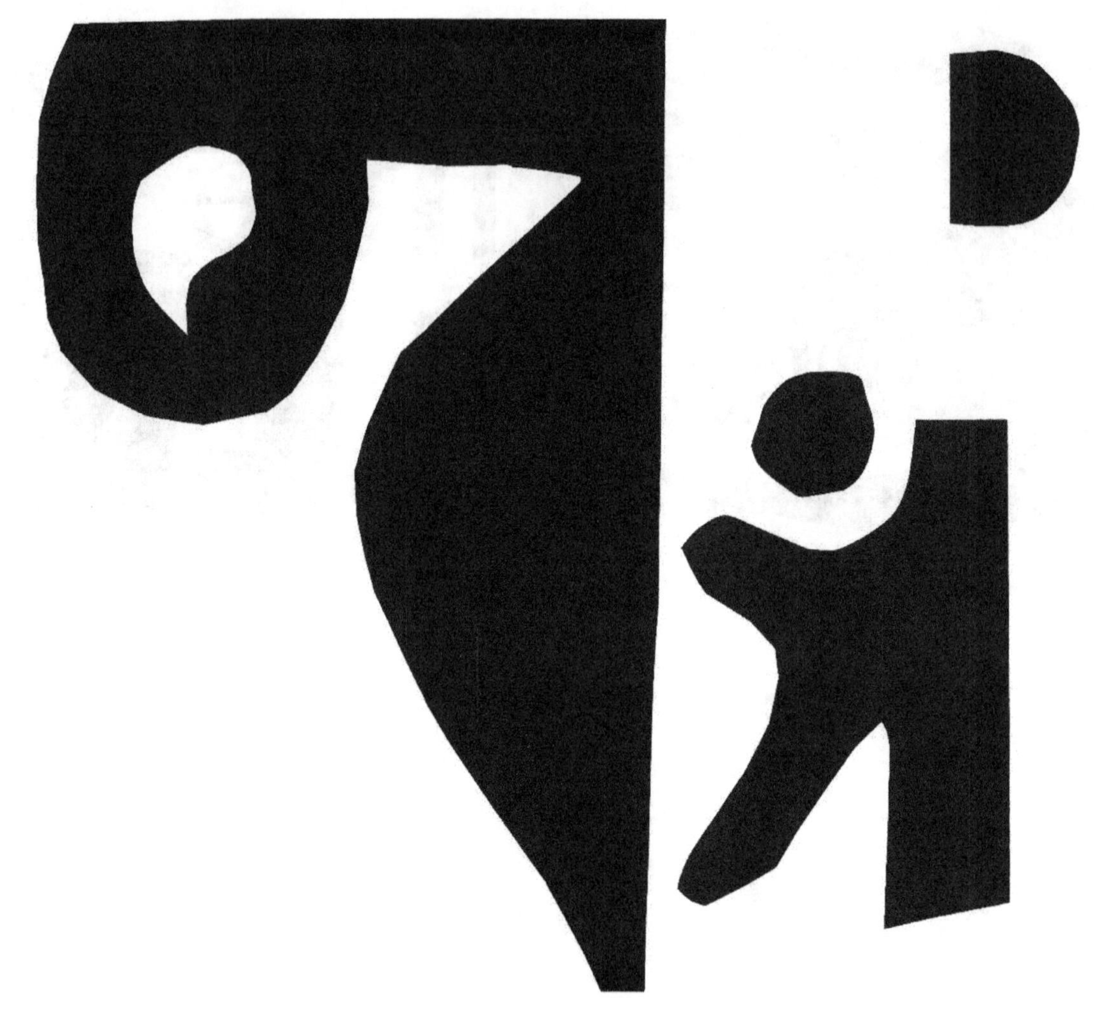

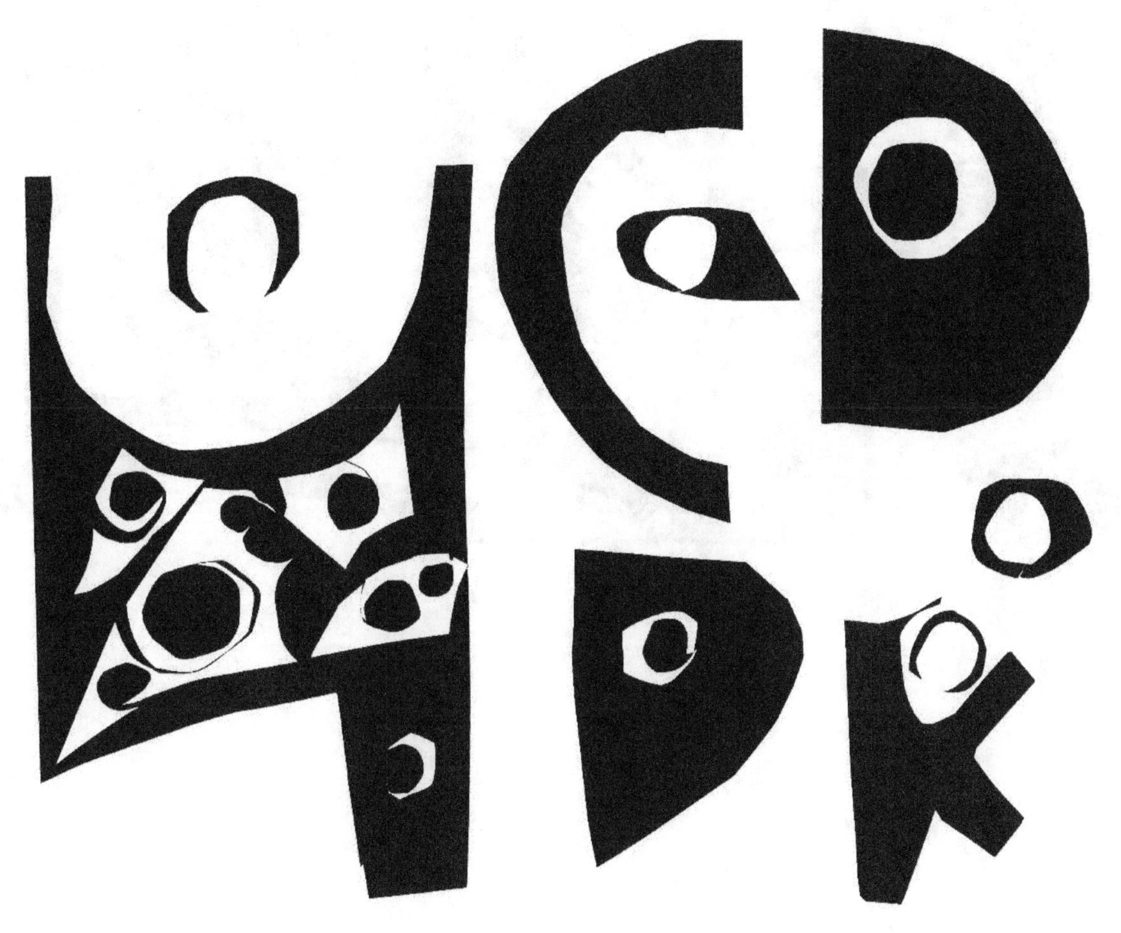

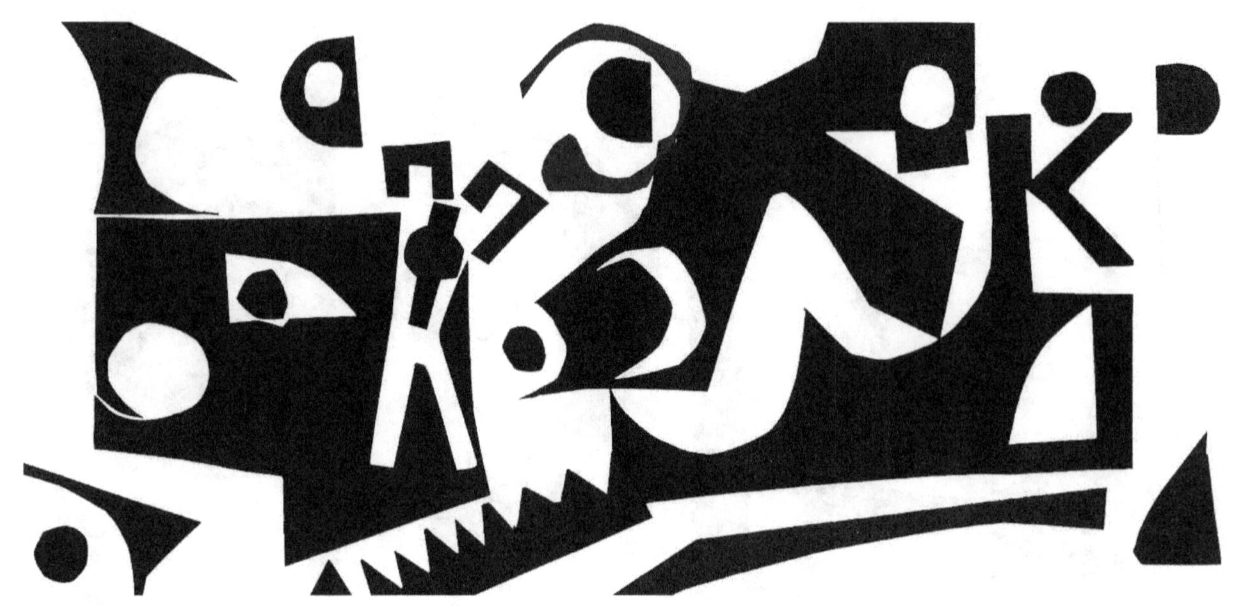

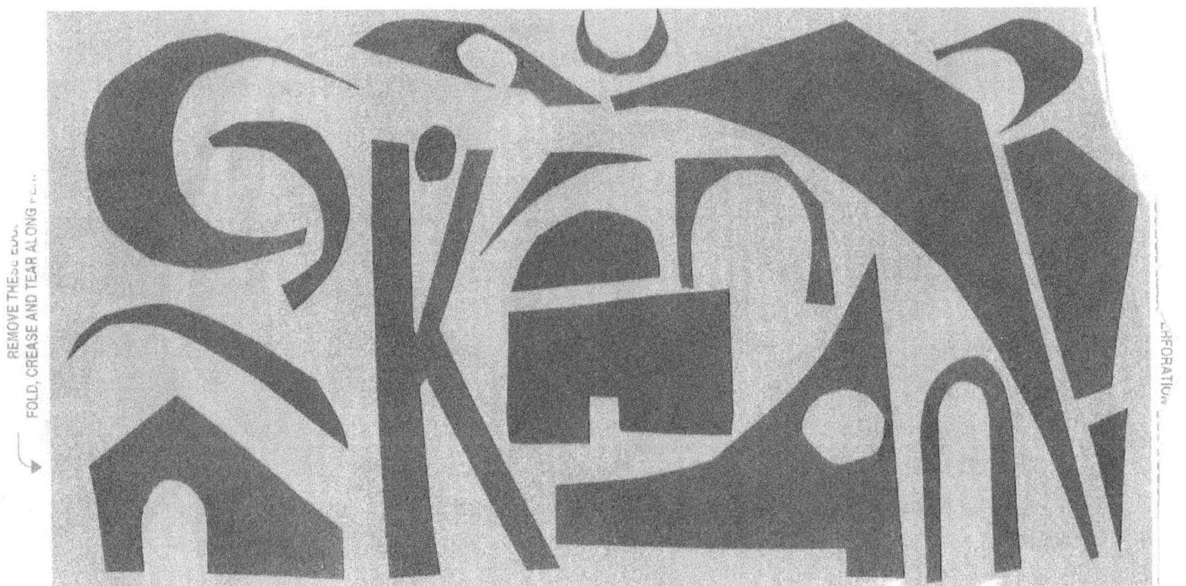

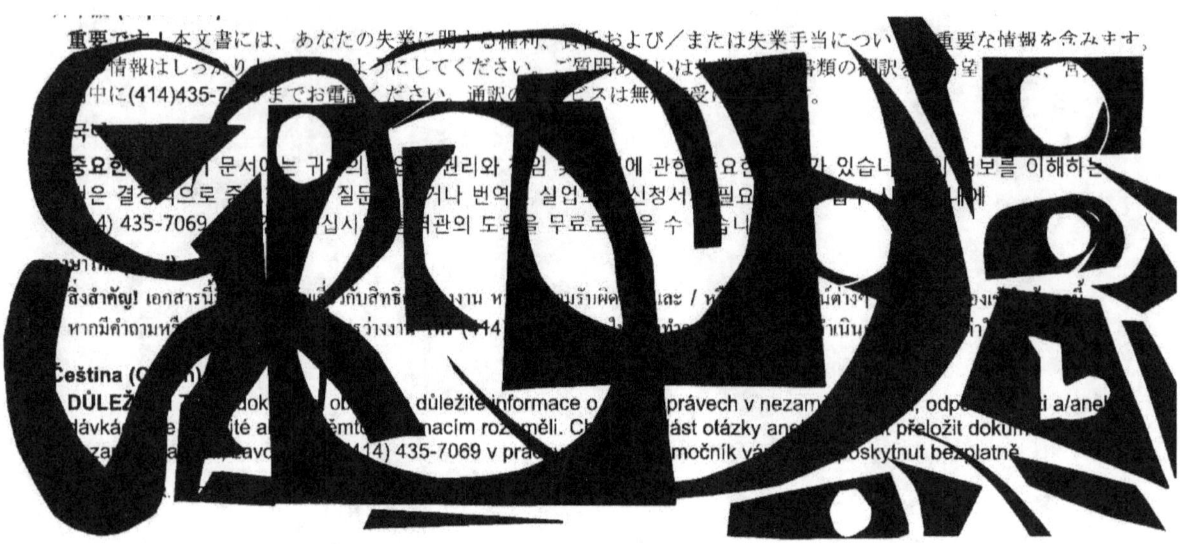

重要です！本文書には、あなたの失業に関する権利、[illegible]および／または失業手当につい[illegible]重要な情報を含みます。
[illegible]情報はしっかり[illegible]ようにしてください。ご質問あ[illegible]いは[illegible]書類の翻訳を[illegible]
[illegible]中に(414)435-7[illegible]までお電話ください。通訳の[illegible]ビスは無[illegible]受[illegible]。

[illegible]국어

중요한[illegible] 문서에는 귀[illegible] 권리와 책임 [illegible]에 관한 [illegible] 있습니[illegible] 정보를 이해하는
[illegible]은 결정[illegible]으로 [illegible] 질문[illegible]거나 번역[illegible] 실업[illegible] 신청서[illegible] 필요[illegible]에
[illegible]4) 435-7069 [illegible]십시[illegible] 관의 도움을 무료로 [illegible]을 수 [illegible]습니[illegible]

สิ่งสำคัญ! เอกสารนี้[illegible]เกี่ยวกับสิทธิ[illegible]งาน [illegible]รับผิด[illegible]และ / [illegible]ต่างๆ [illegible]
หากมีคำถามหรือ[illegible]ว่างงาน [illegible] (414) [illegible]

Čeština (Č[illegible])

DŮLEŽ[illegible] dok[illegible] ob[illegible] důležité informace o [illegible] právech v nezam[illegible], odp[illegible] a/anebo
dávká[illegible] ité a[illegible] těmto [illegible]macím rozuměli. Ch[illegible] ást otázky ane[illegible] přeložit dokum[illegible]
[illegible]zav[illegible] (414) 435-7069 v prác[illegible] pomocník vá[illegible] poskytnut bezplatně

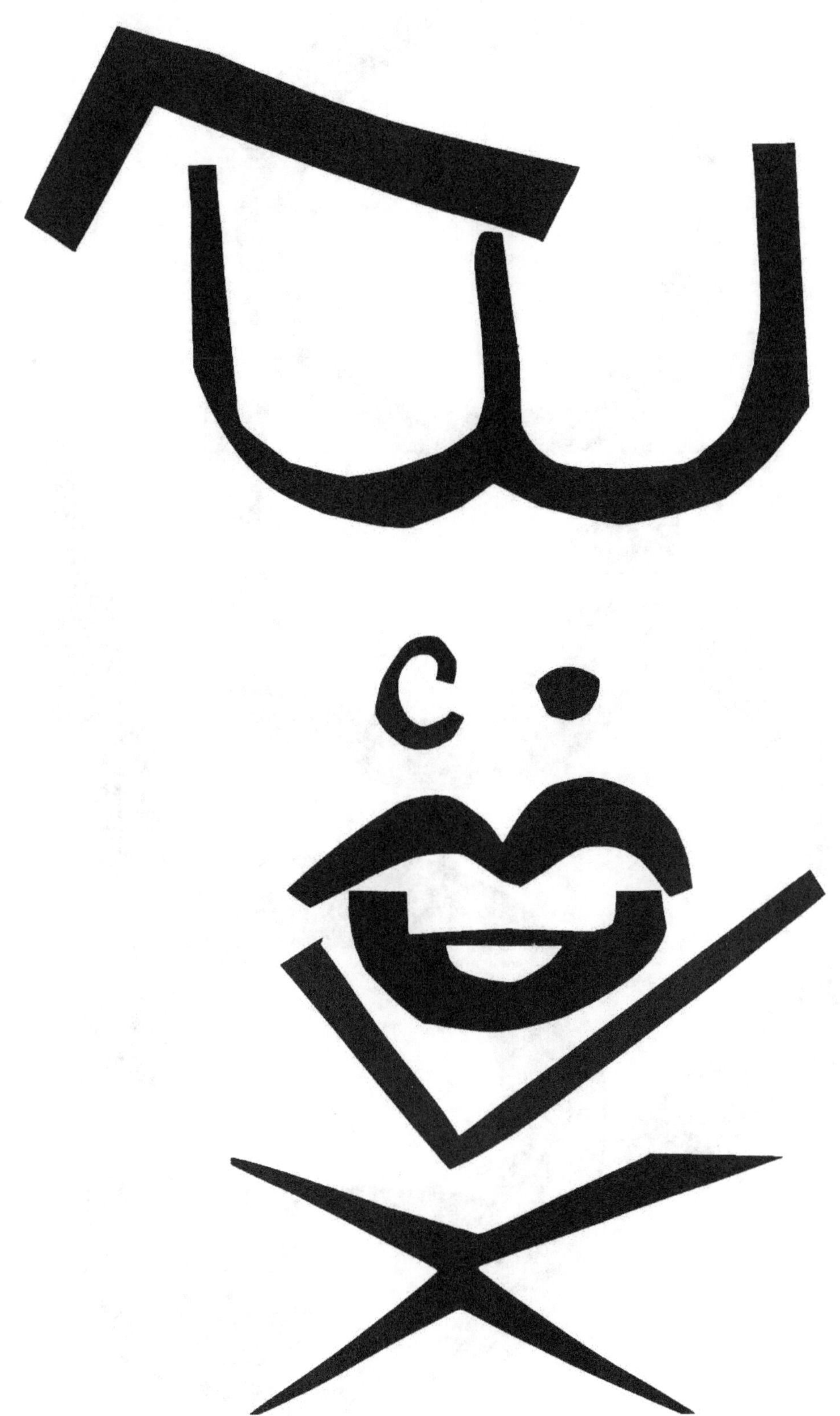

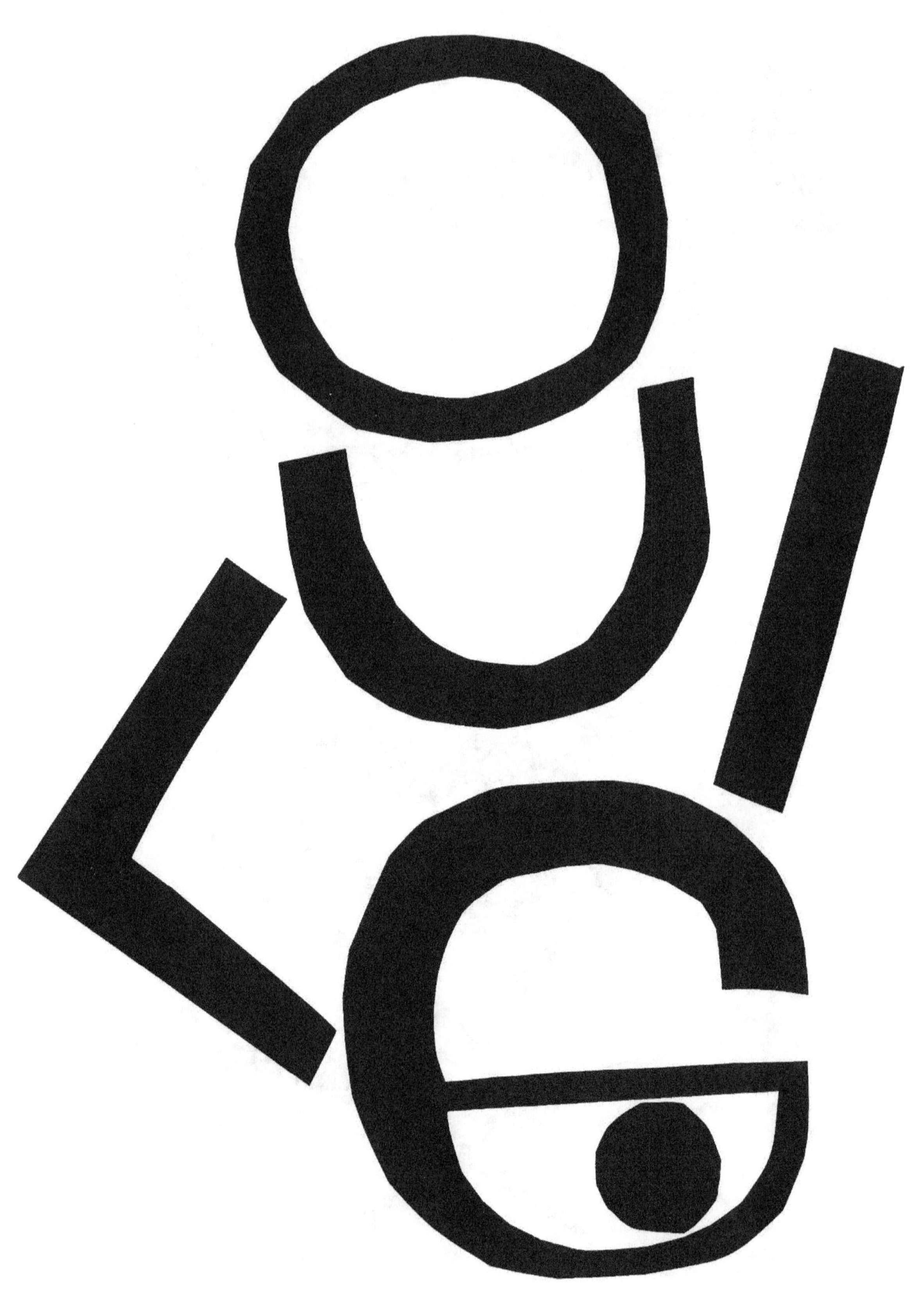

documents de chômage, appelez le (414) 435-7069 pendant les heures ouvrables
gracieusement par un interprète.

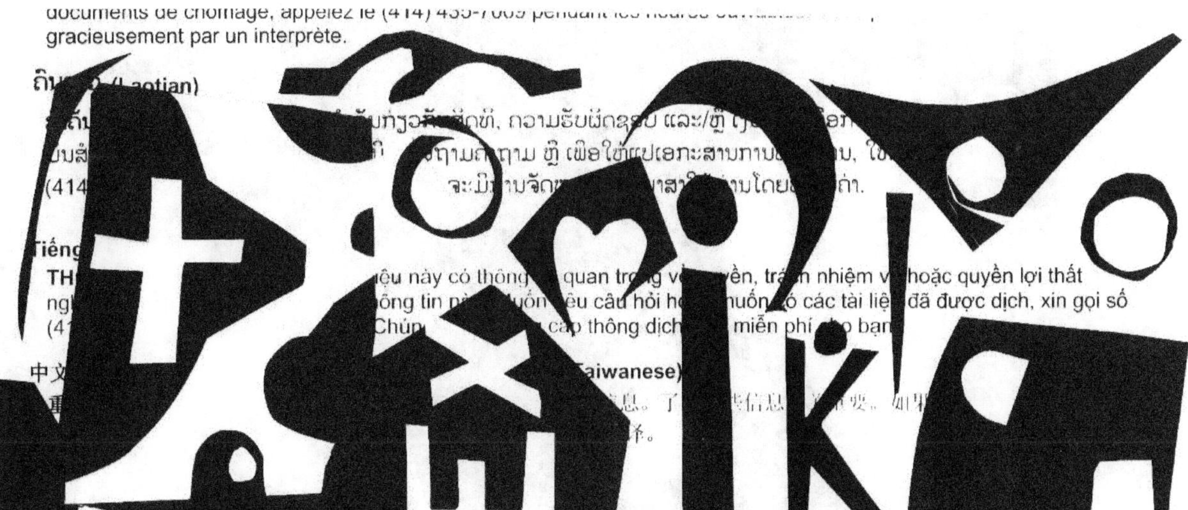

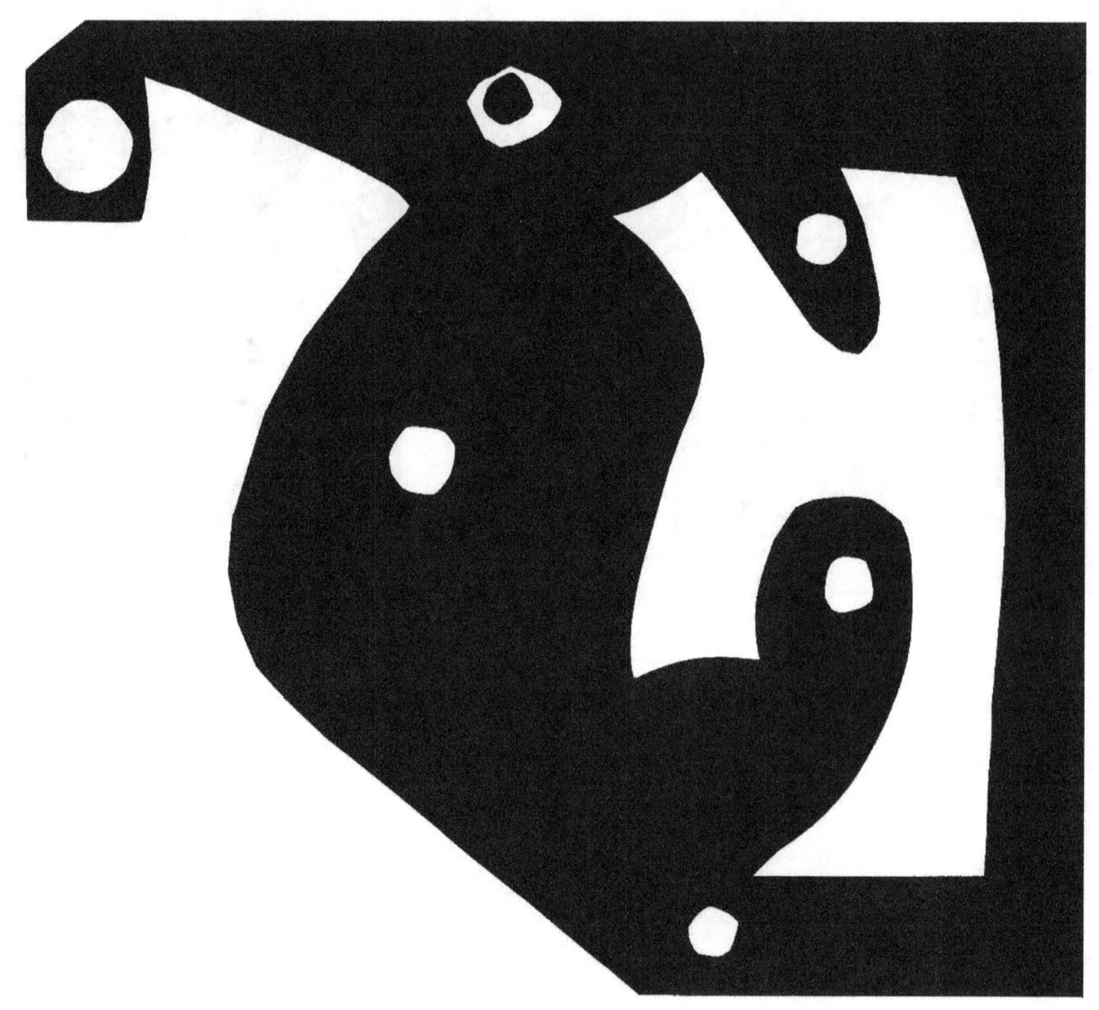

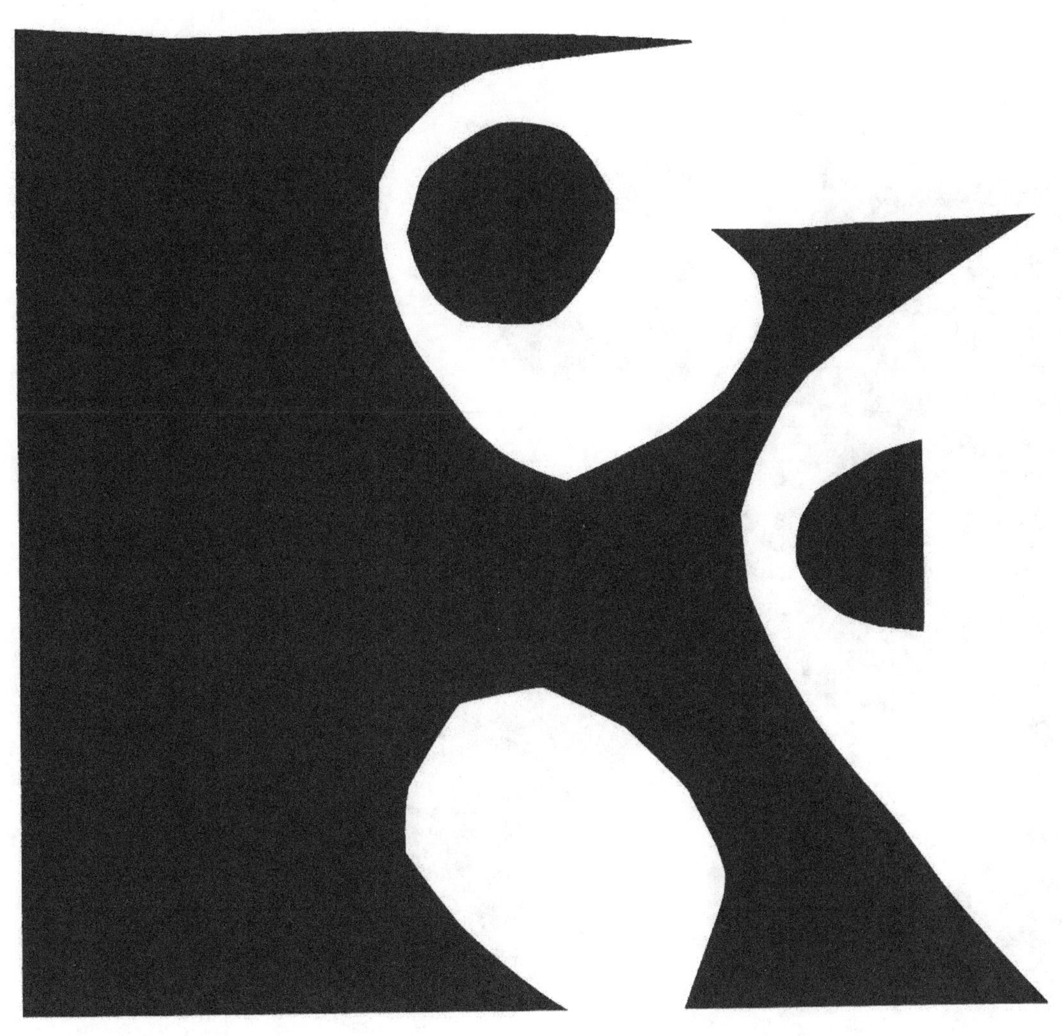

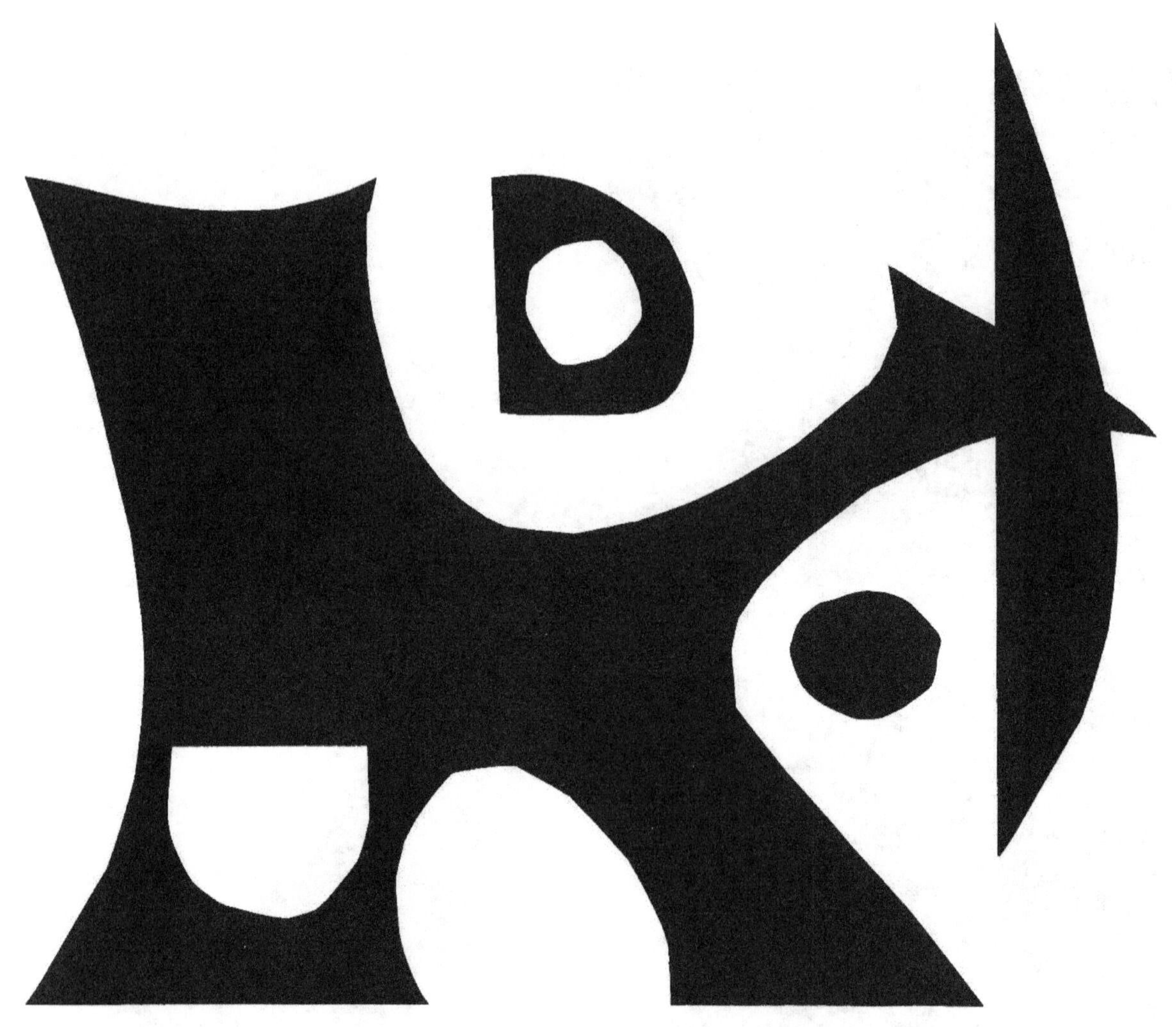

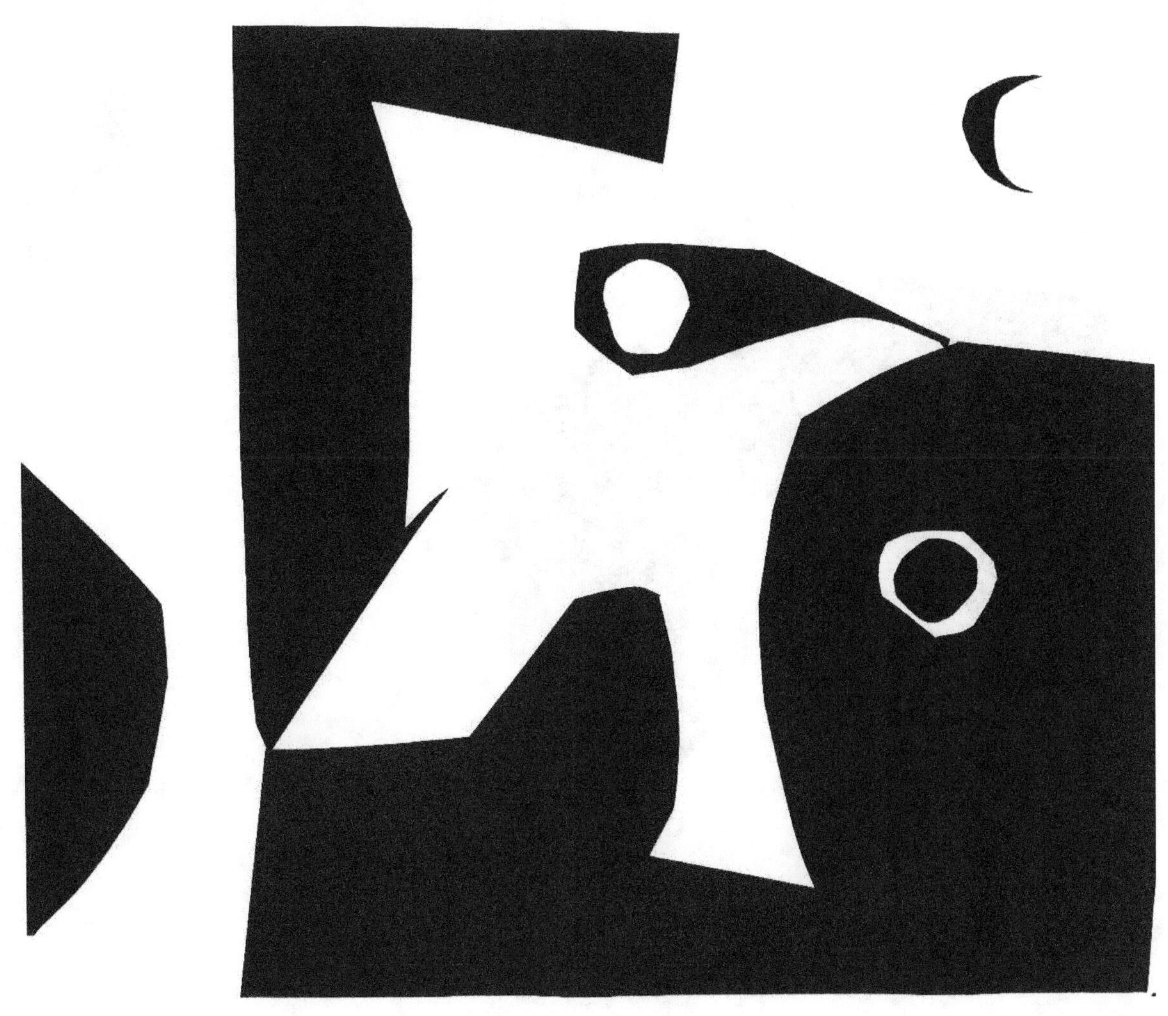

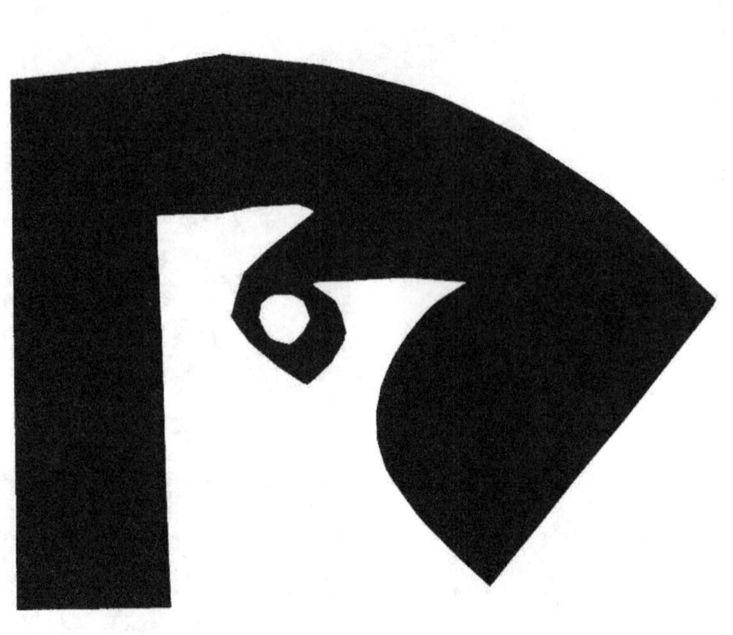

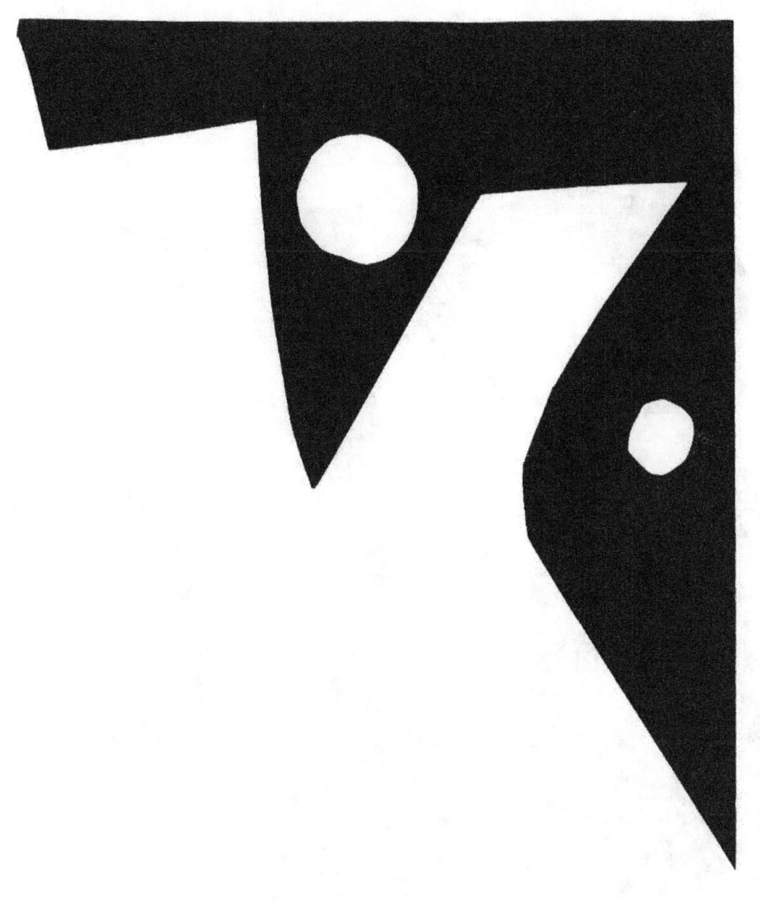

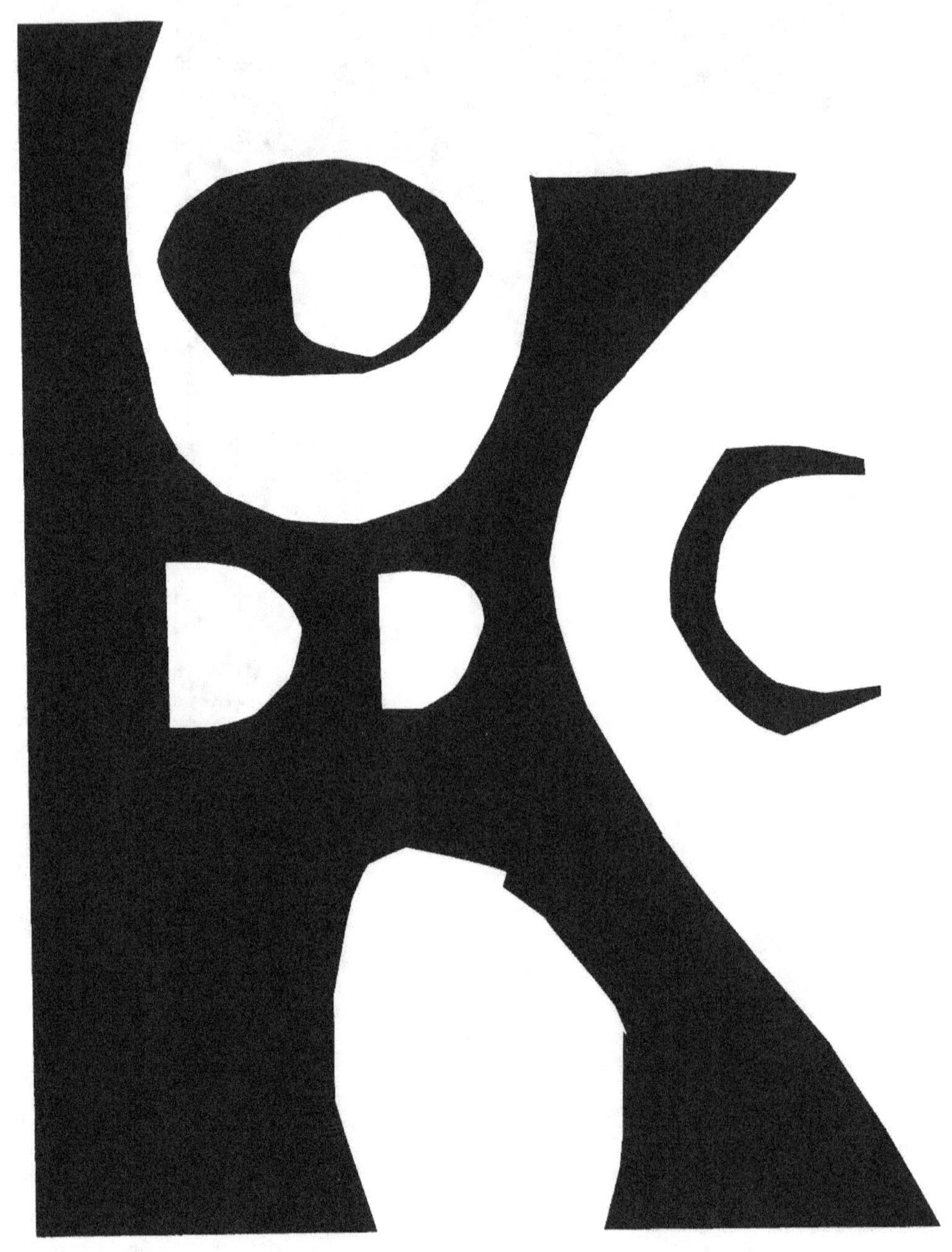

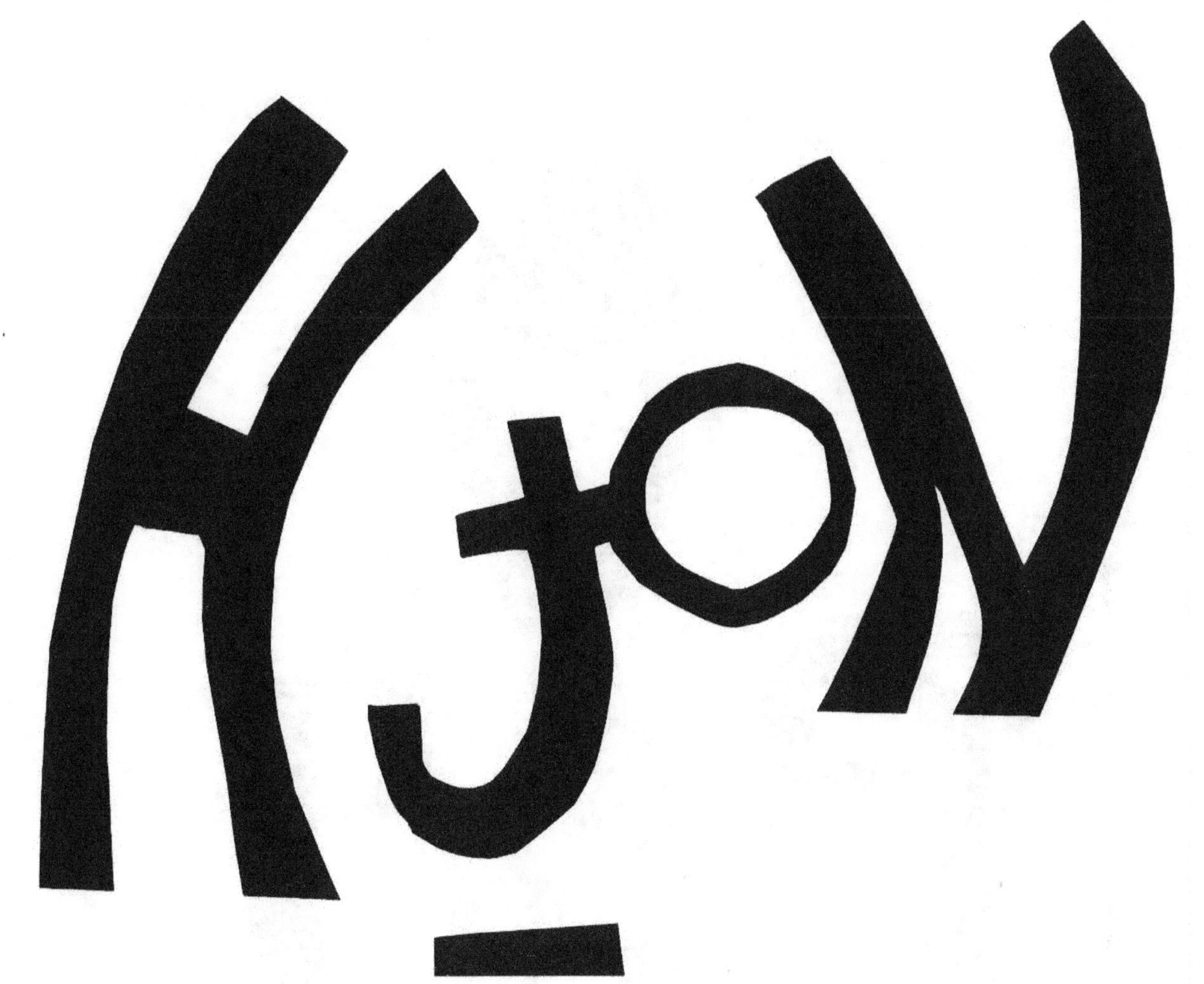

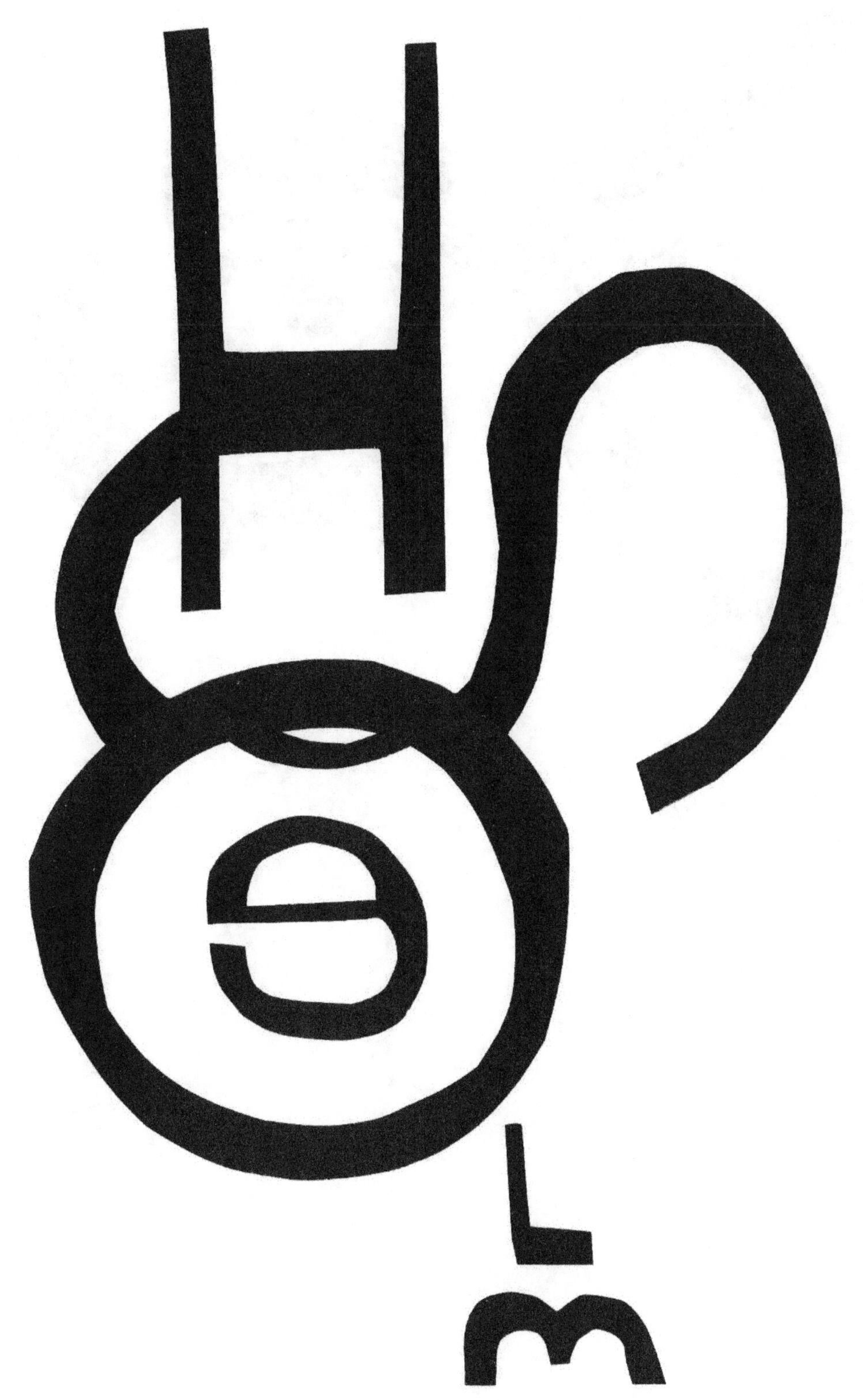

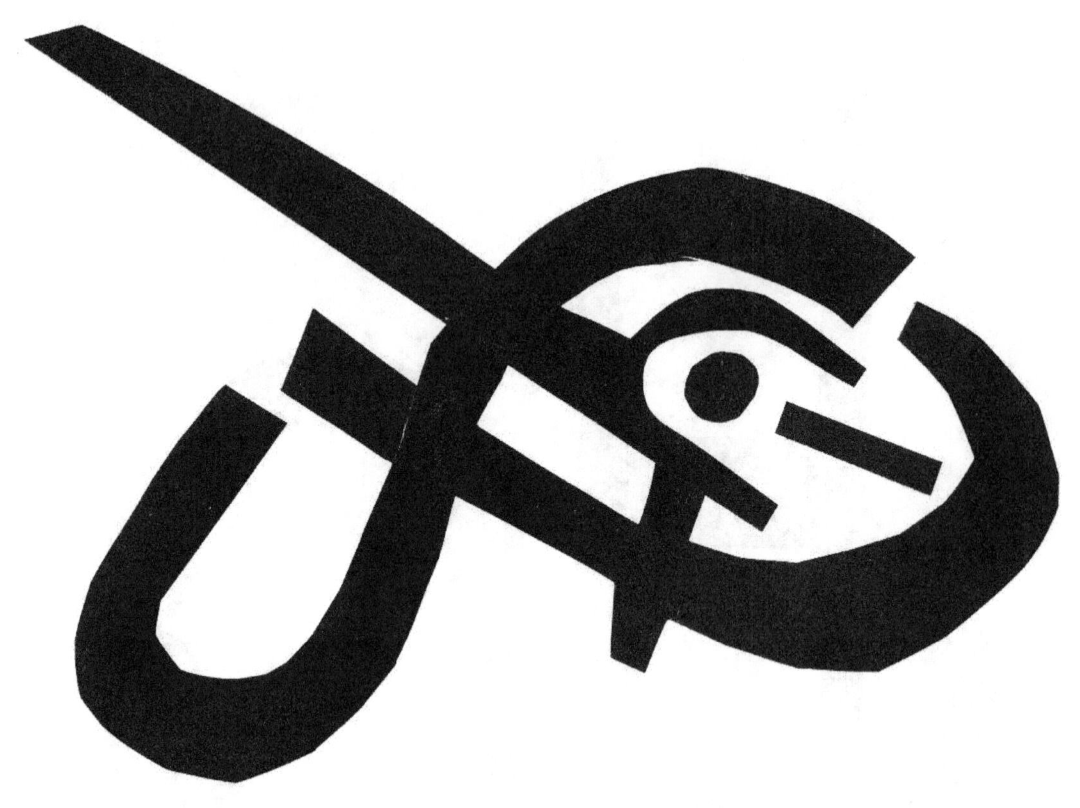

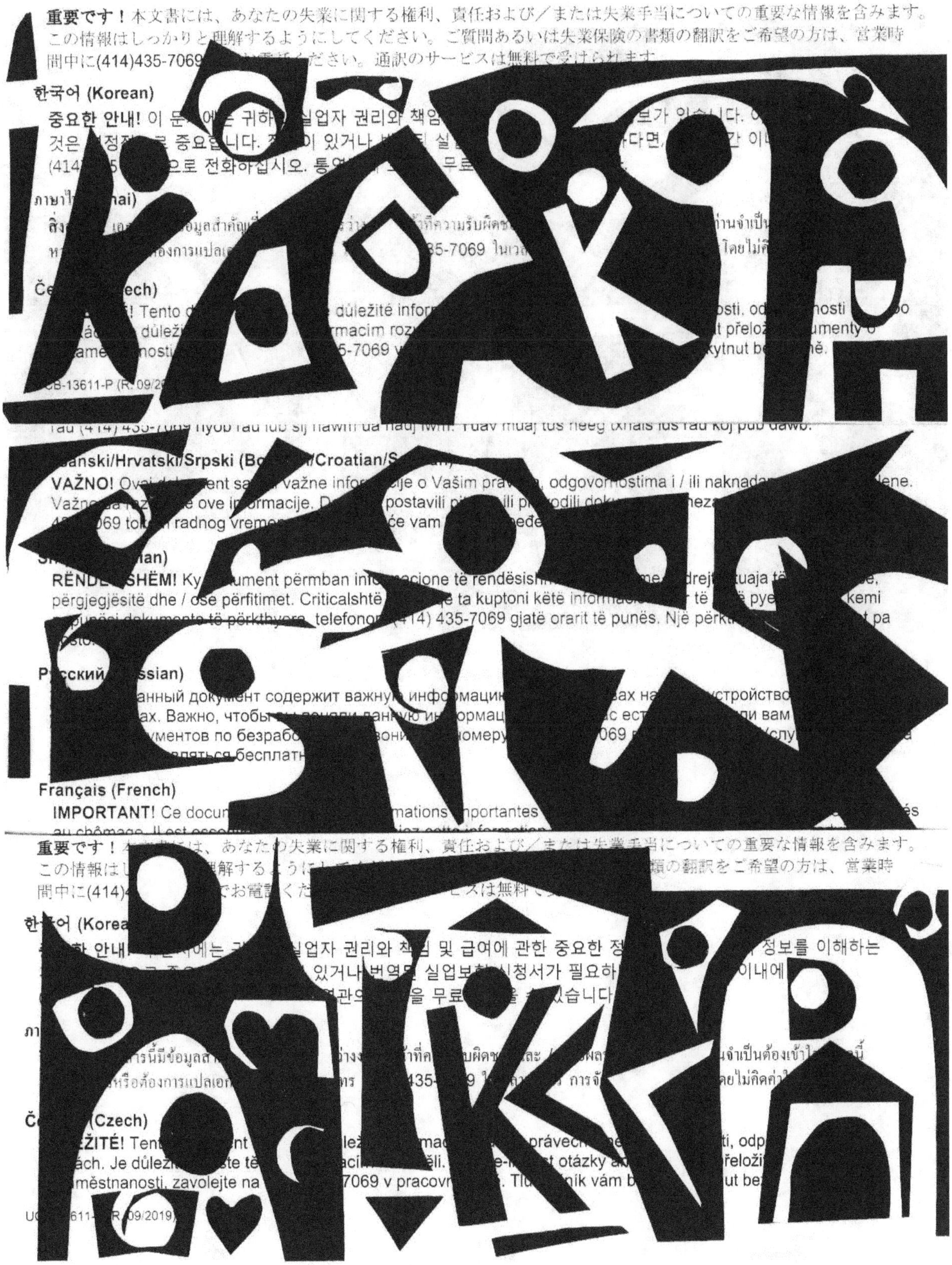

重要です！本文書には、あなたの失業に関する権利、責任および／または失業手当についての重要な情報を含みます。
この情報はしっかりと理解するようにしてください。ご質問あるいは失業保険の書類の翻訳をご希望の方は、営業時
間中に(414)435-7069 ... 通訳のサービスは無料で受けられます

한국어 (Korean)

중요한 안내! 이 문 ... 에는 귀하 ... 실업자 권리와 책임 ... 보가 있습니다.
것은 ... 정 ... 로 중요합니다. ... 이 있거나 ... 실 ... 다면, ... 간 이내
(414) ... 5 ... 으로 전화하십시오. 통역 ... 무료

ภาษาไ ... hai)

... 435-7069 ในเวล ... โดยไม่คิ

Če ... ech)

... ! Tento d ... důležité infor ... osti, od ... nosti ... bo
... důleži ... rmacím roz ... t přelož ... umenty o
... nosti ... 5-7069 v ... kytnut be ... ně.

... B-13611-P (R. 09/20

rau (414) 435-7069 hyob rau lub sij hawm ua hauj lwm. Yuav muaj tus neeg txhais lus rau koj pub dawb.

... anski/Hrvatski/Srpski (Bo ... /Croatian/S ...

VAŽNO! Ovaj do ... ent sa ... važne info ... cije o Vašim pra ... , odgovornostima i / ili naknada ... lene.
Važno ... ove informacije. ... postavili pi ... ili prevodili doku ... neza
43 ... 069 to ... radnog vreme ... će vam ... eđe

Sh ... an)

RËNDE ... SHËM! Ky ... ument përmban info ... cione të rëndësish ... drej ... tuaja të ... e,
përgjegjësitë dhe / ose përfitimet. Criticalshtë ... e ta kuptoni këtë informac ... të ... pye ... kemi
... të përkthyera, telefono ... (414) 435-7069 gjatë orarit të punës. Një përkt ... t pa
... sto.

Русский ... sian)

... анный документ содержит важную инфо ... мацию ... ах на ... устройство
... ах. Важно, чтобы ... данную ин ... рмац ... с есть ... ли вам
... ументов по безрабо ... вони ... номеру ... 069 ... /слу ... а
... бесплатн

Français (French)

IMPORTANT! Ce docu ... mations importantes ... és
au chômage. Il est essent ... iez cette information

重要です！本 ... は、あなたの失業に関する権利、責任および／または失業手当についての重要な情報を含みます。
この情報はし ... 理解するように ... 類の翻訳をご希望の方は、営業時
間中に(414)4 ... でお電話くださ ... ビスは無料で

한국어 (Korea

... 한 안내! ... 에는 ... 실업자 권리와 책임 및 급여에 관한 중요한 정 ... 정보를 이해하는
... 있거나 번역된 실업보험 신청서가 필요하 ... 이내에
... 관의 ... 을 무료 ... 습니다

ภา

... การนี้มีข้อมูลสำ ... ที่ค ... บผิดช ... และ ... จำเป็นต้องเข้าใ
... หรือต้องการแปลเอก ... 435- ... 9 ... การจั ... ดยไม่คิดค่า

Če ... (Czech)

... ŽITÉ! Tent ... nt ... ležit ... mac ... právech ... ti, odp
... ách. Je důlež ... ste tě ... ací ... ěli. ... t otázky ... řeloži
... městnanosti, zavolejte na ... 7069 v pracov ... Tlu ... ník vám b ... ut be

UC ... 611- ... R. 09/2019)

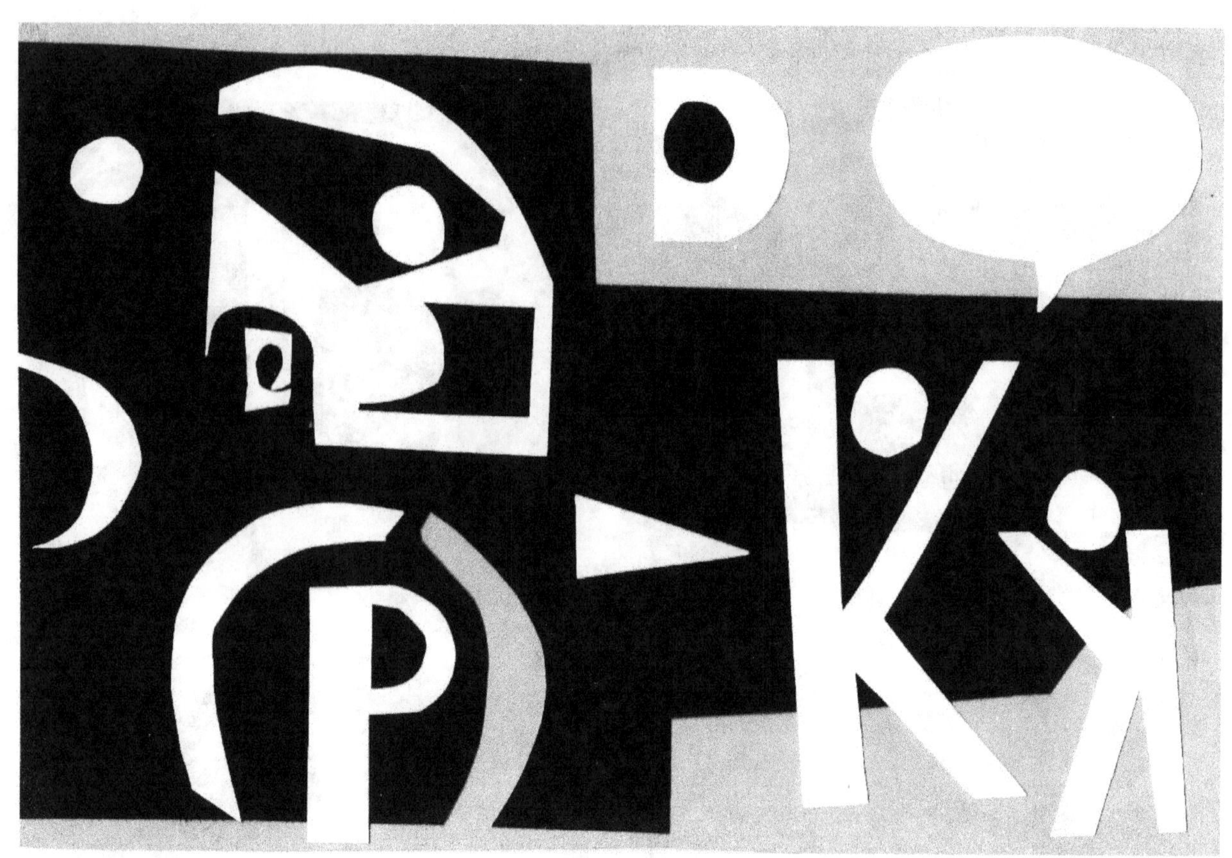

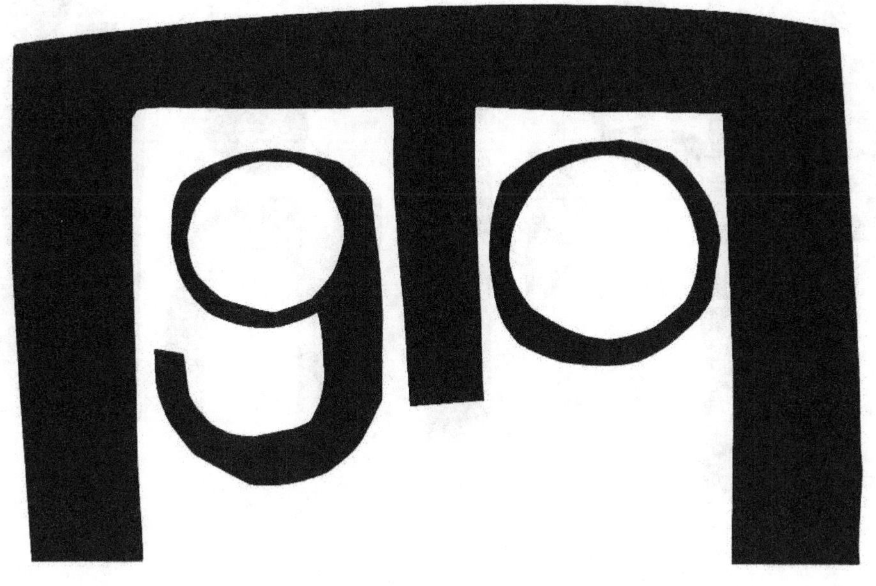

drink

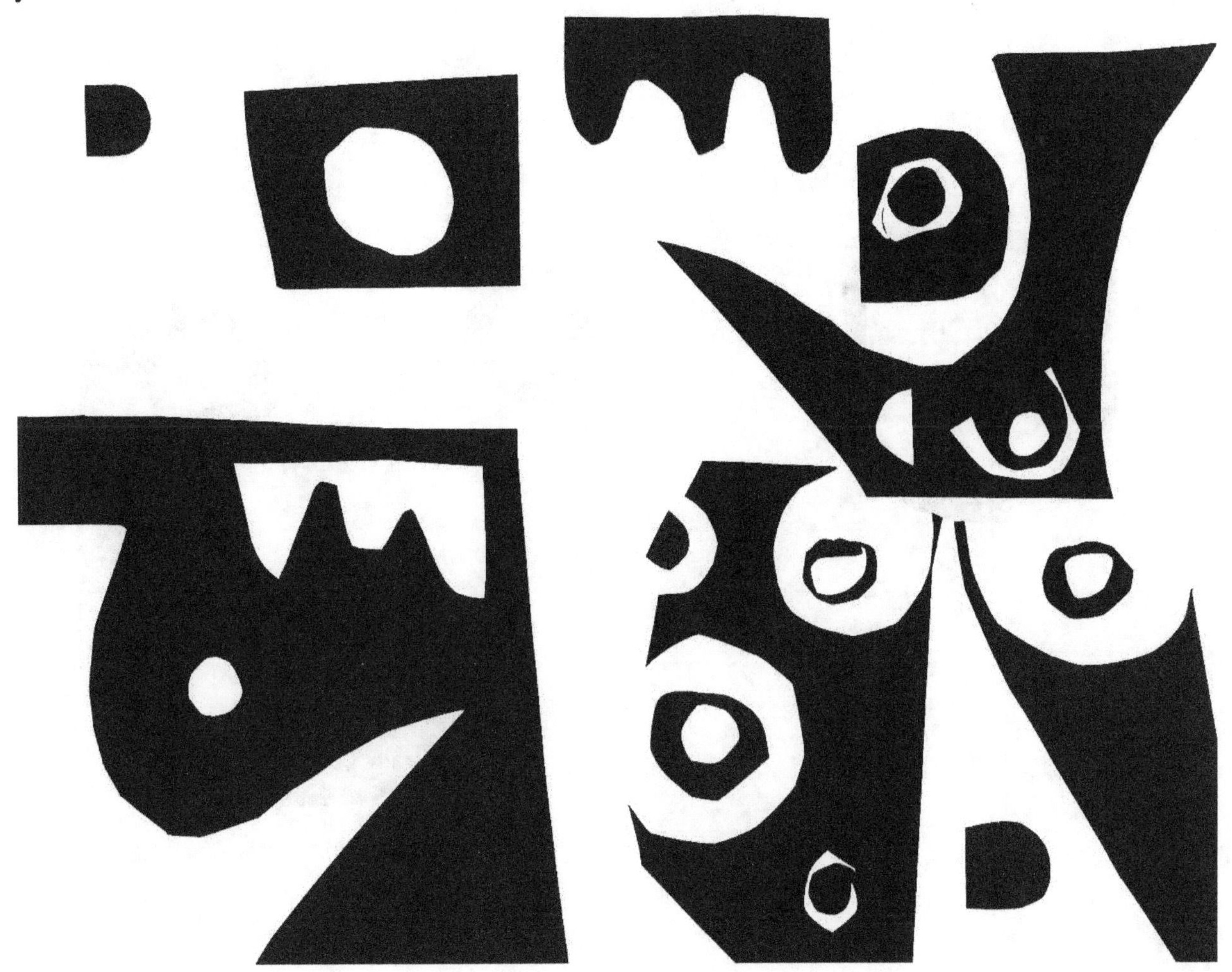

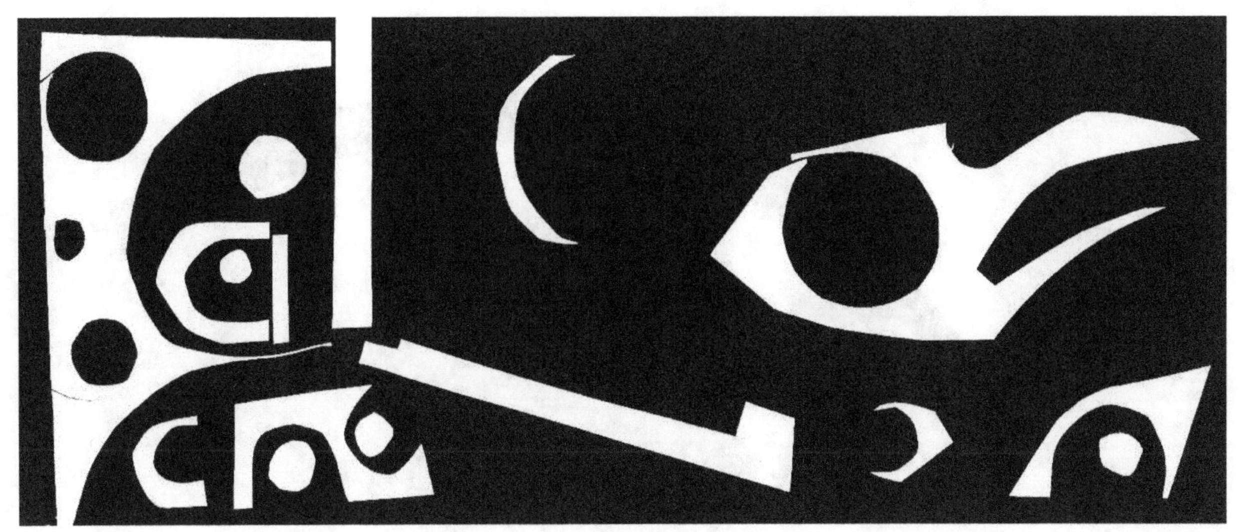

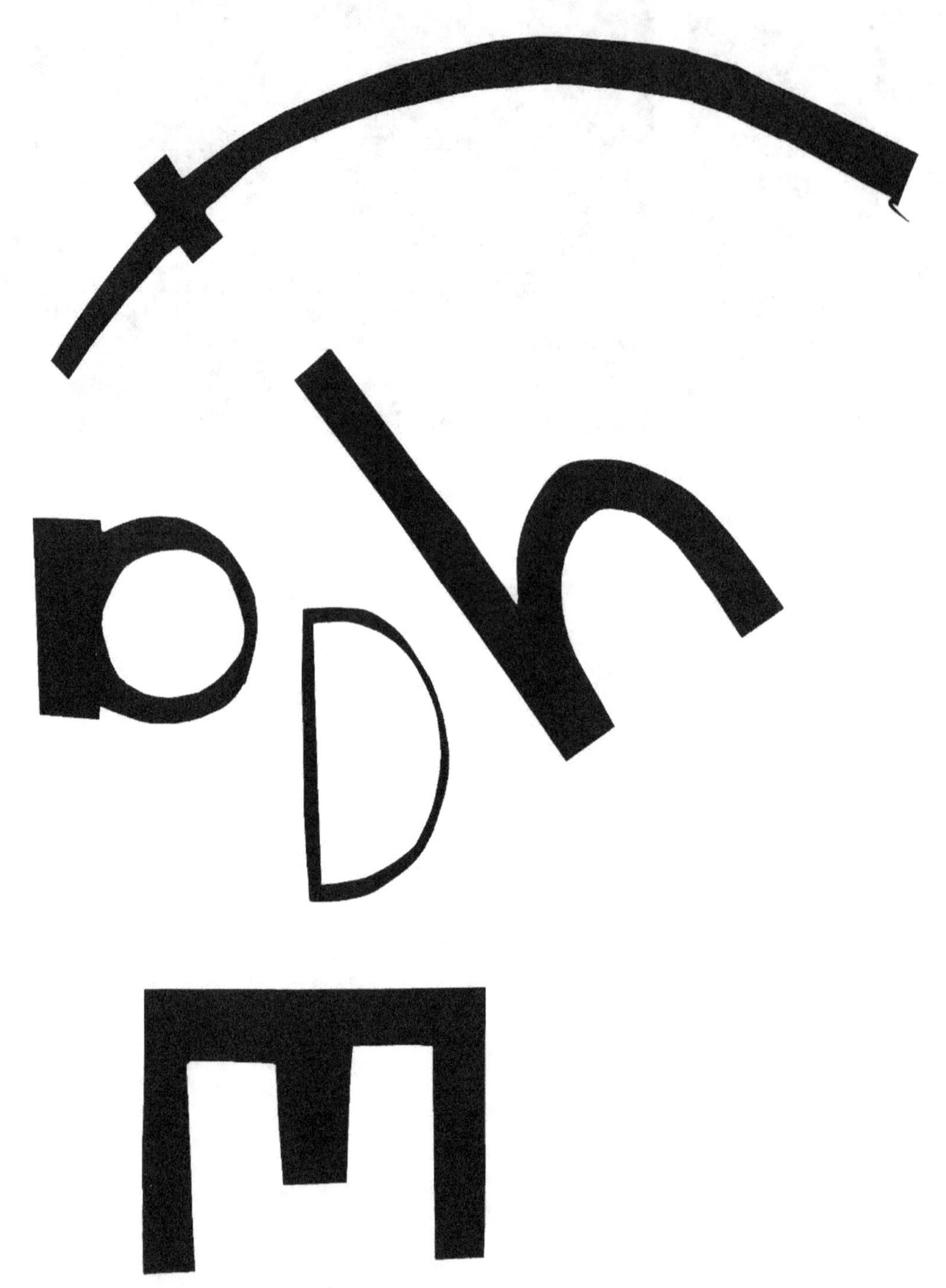

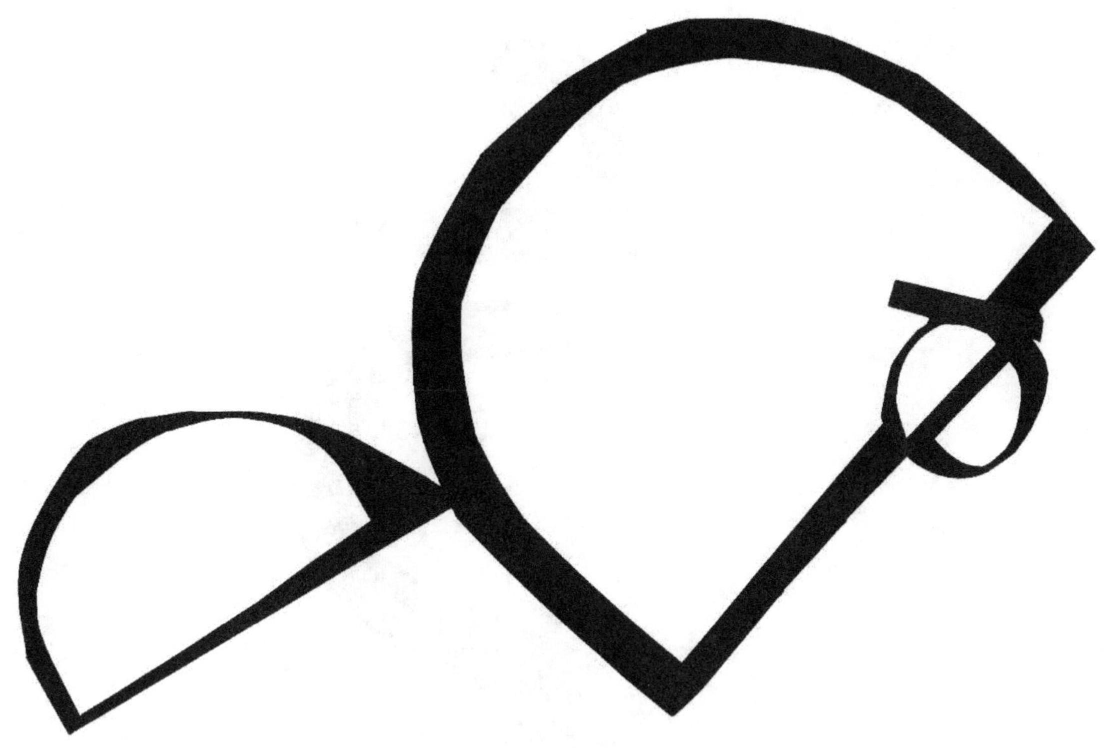

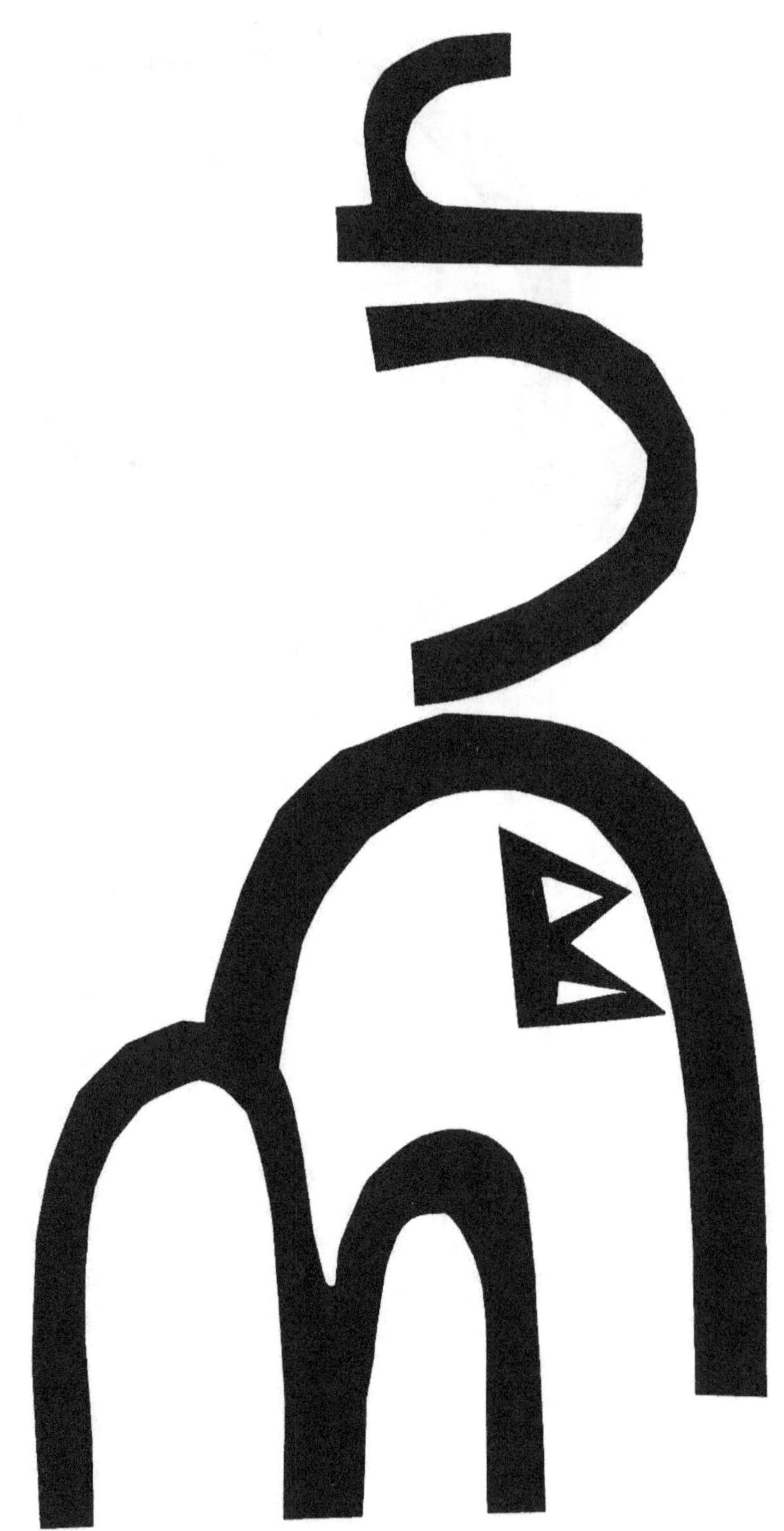

¢off.e.e

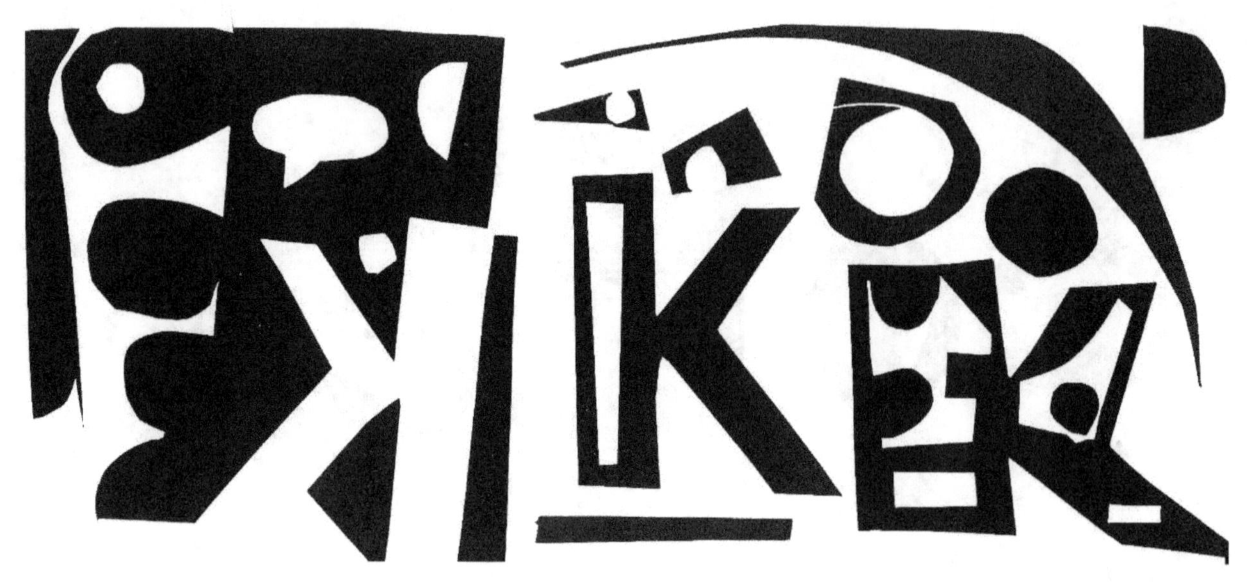

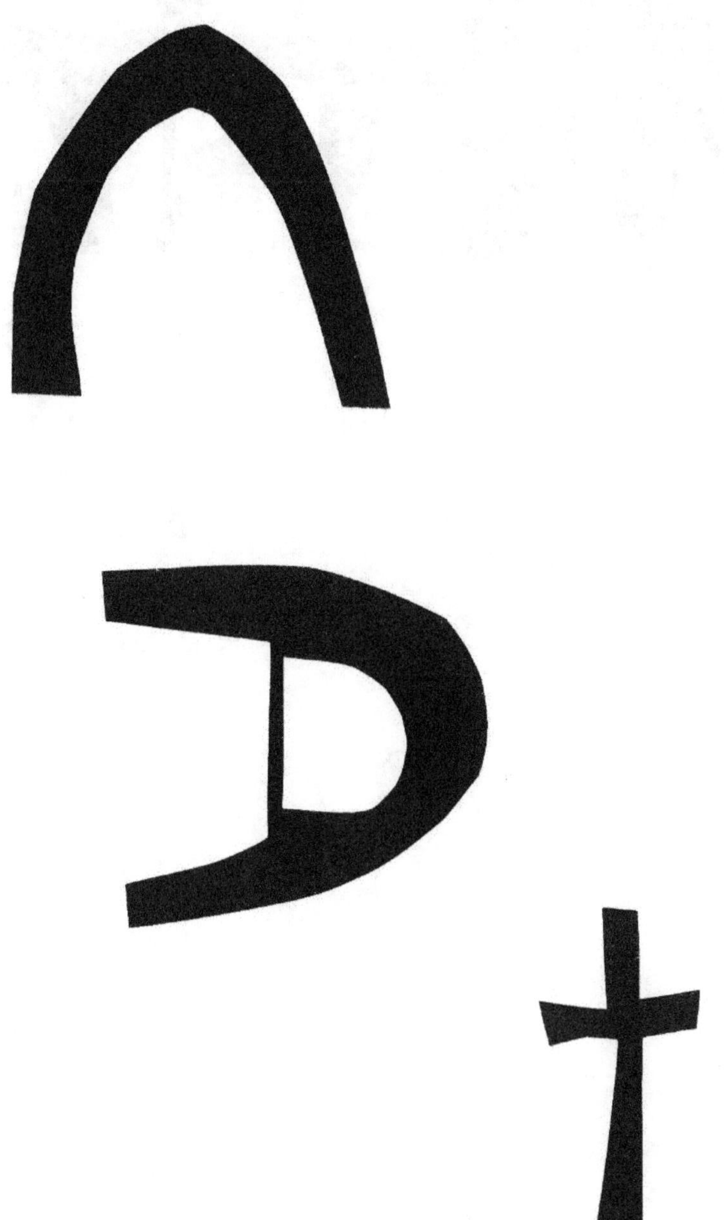

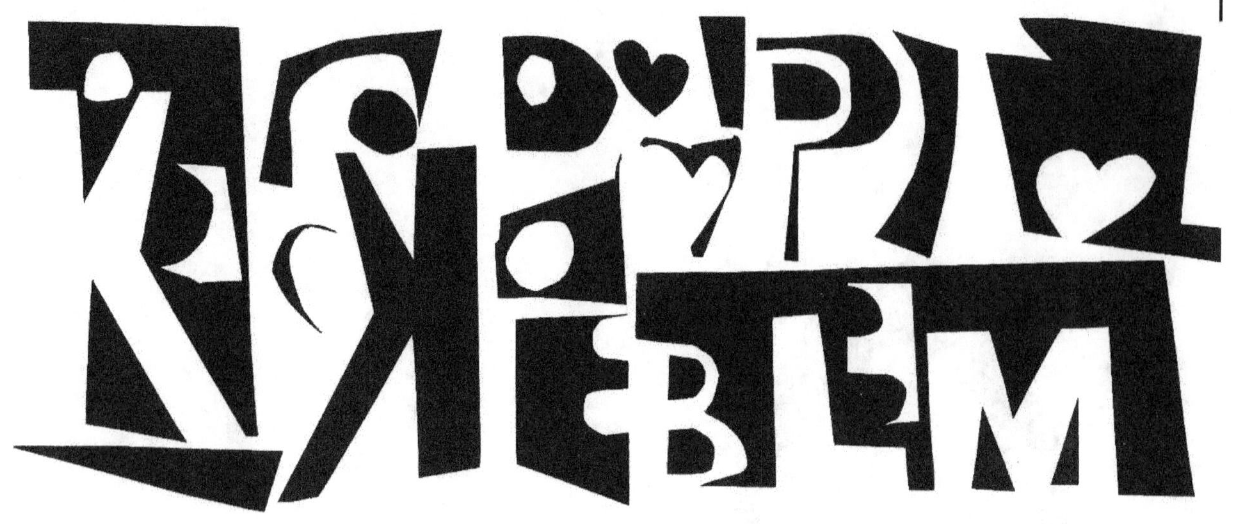

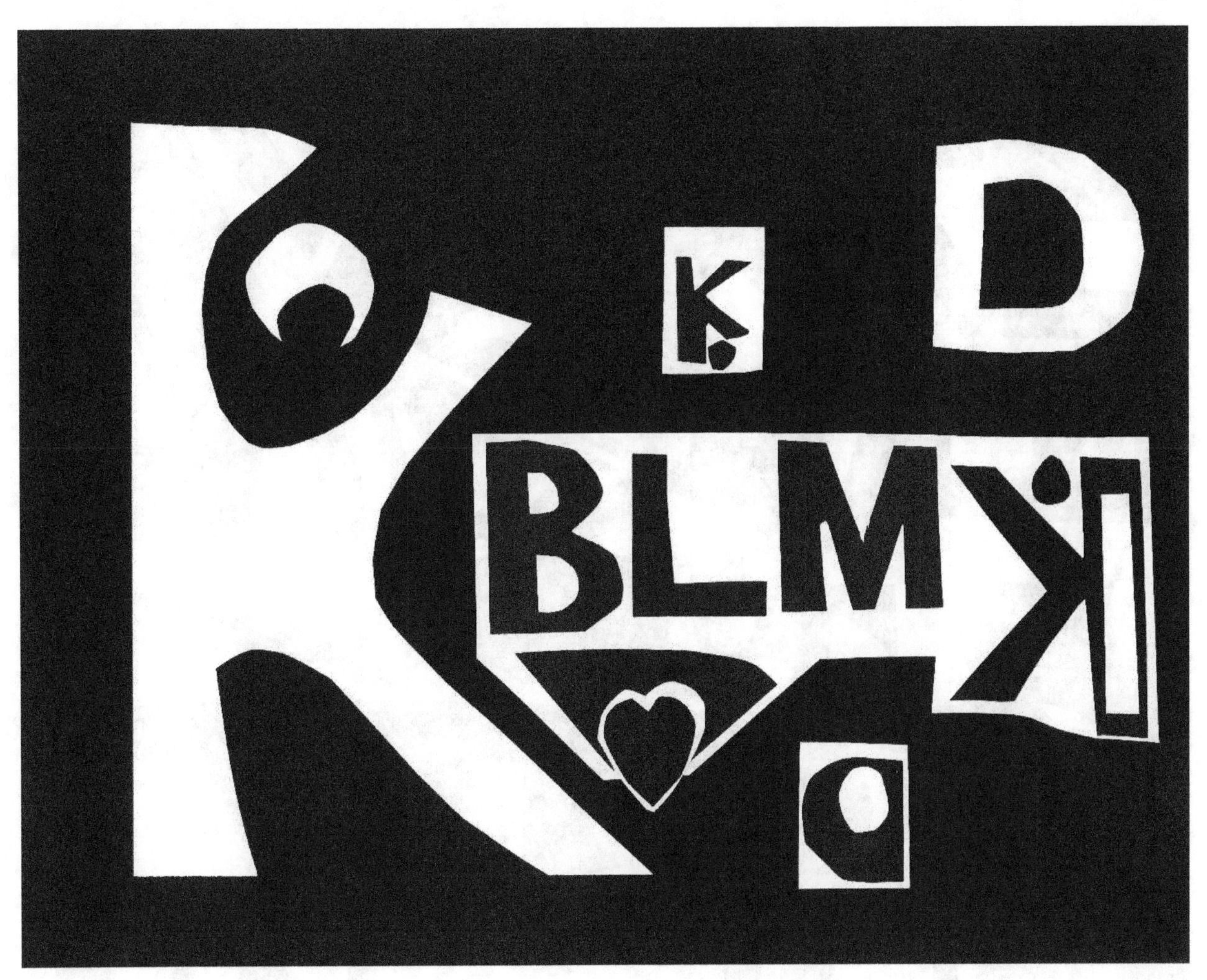
K
D
BLM

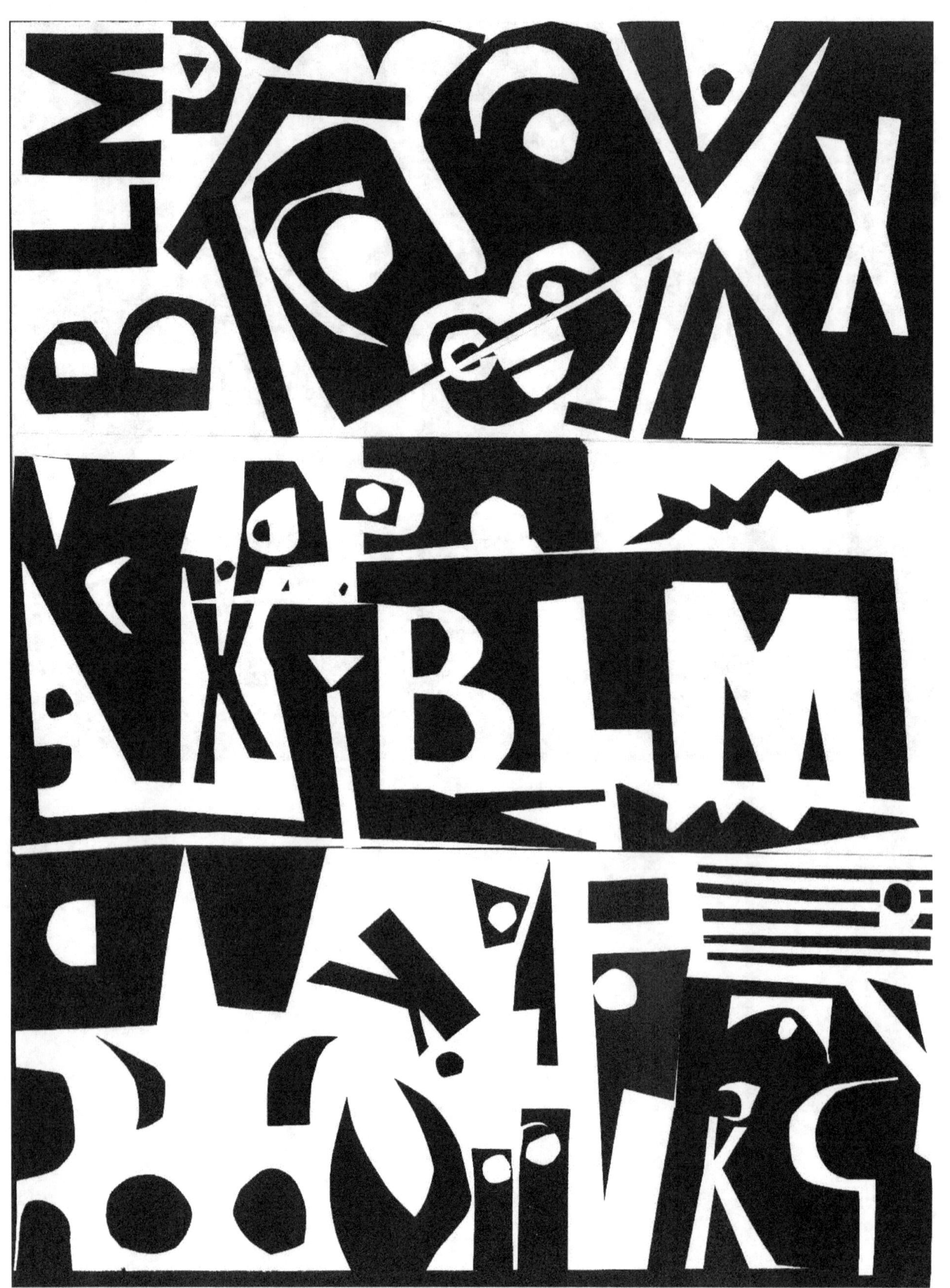
BLM

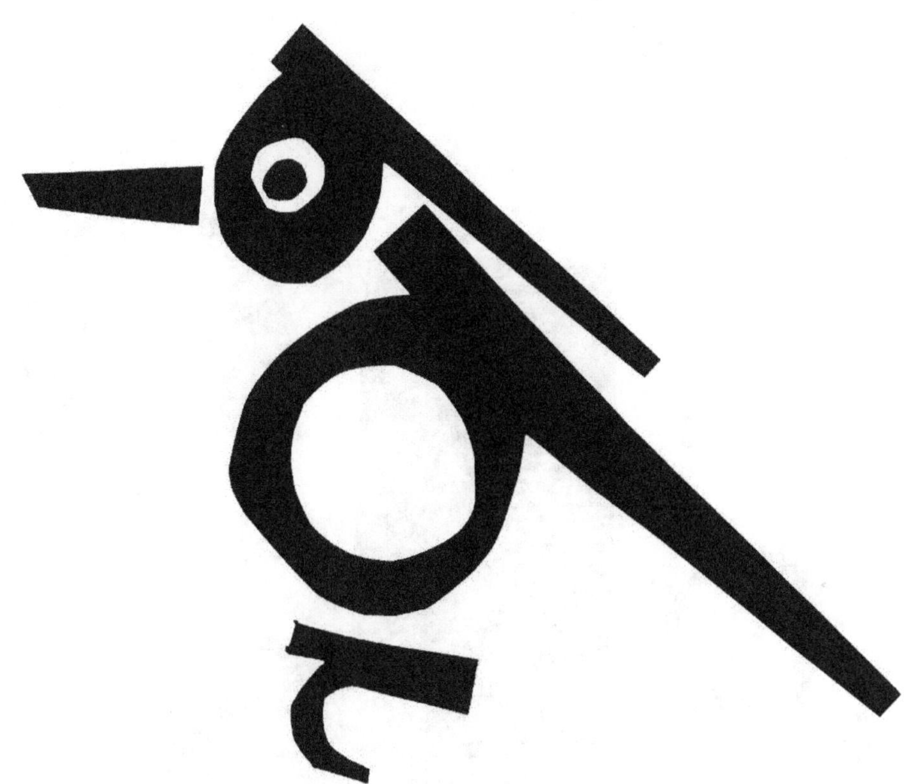

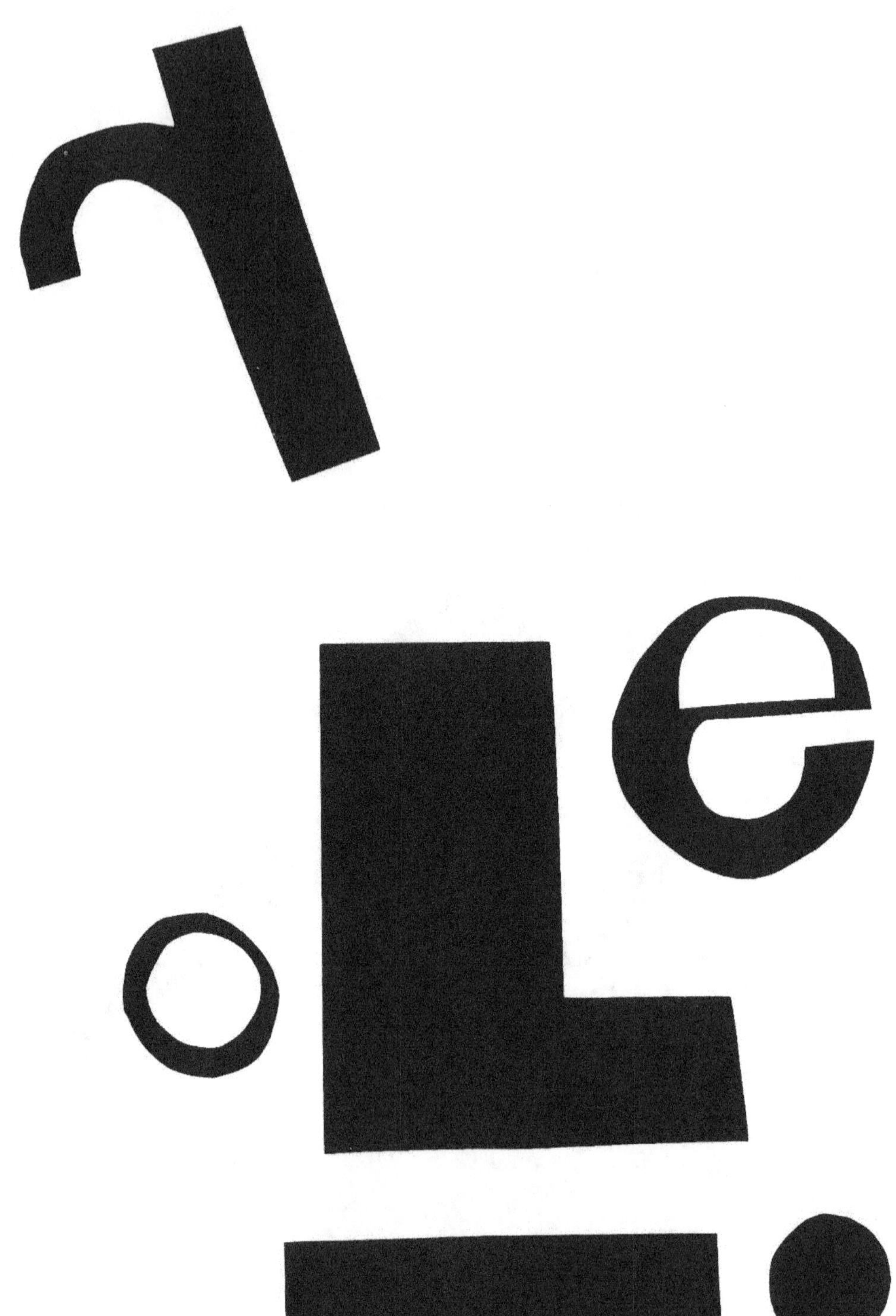

a

B B

u U

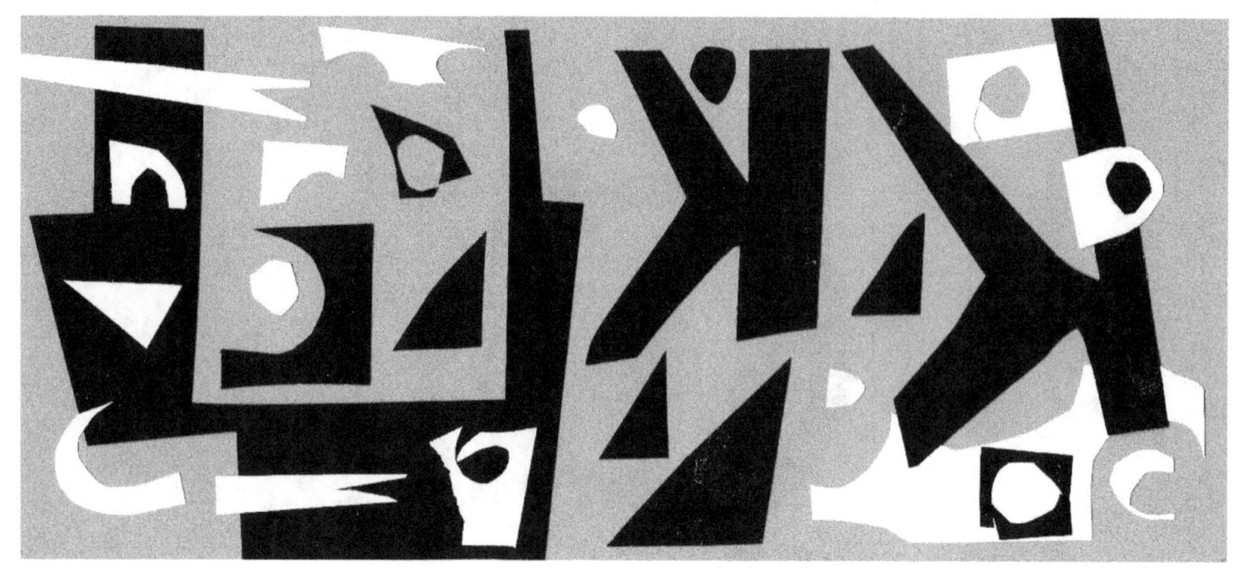

u lub sij hawm ua hauj lwm. Yuav muaj tus neeg txhais lus rau koj pub dawb.

sanski/ orpski (Bosr roatian/Serb

VAŽNO! O dokum sadrži važne informac slene.
Važno da razumete formacije. D postavili p (414)
435-7069 t om radn re na. Prevodila će vam biti obe

ument përmban infor ëndësishme me të dreit ë papur ë,
et. Criticalshtë k uptoni këtë i cion. P etje ose mi
pa unë okumente të p era, telefononi 069 gjatë orar unës s do t'i t pa
kost

сский Rus n)

ВАЖНО й док держи ажную инфор ию о ва х п строй стях
и/или ль ажно ы поня данную инфор ию. ли у или
перево до нтов отице, звоните по ном 435- асы. чика
будут едо лять сп но.

Franç (Fren)

IMPORTANT! Ce document contient des rmations im tant ur vo ou avantages lié
chômage. Il est omprenez cette ation. Pour
documents de chôm

重要です！本文書には あなたの失 び／または失業手当
しっかり 理解するよう てくださ るいは失業保険の書
中に(4 435-70 までお電話く 通訳の 無料 受けられます。

한국어 (Kore)

중요한 안내! 이 문 에는 귀하의 실 권리와 책임 및 에 관한 중요 있습니
것은 결정적 서가 무 시
오. 통역관의 수 있

ภาษาไทย (Thai)

เกี่ยวกับสิทธิการว่างงาน หน้าที่
สารการว่างงาน โทร (414) 435-

tina (Czech)

DŮLEŽITÉ! Ten ent je důležité informace práve ov /aneb
vkách. Je důle ste t informacím rozuměli. Ch ást d do o
n zaměstnanosti te na (414) 435-7069 v pracovní d moc plat

UCB- 11-P (R. 09/201

(414) 435-7069

ខ្មែរ (Khmer/Cambodian)

សំខាន់! ឯកសារនេះមានផ្ទុក ព័ត៌មានសំខាន់អំពីសិទ្ធិ ការទទួលខុសត្រូវ ឬអត្ថប្រយោ

glalaman ormasyon tungkol sa atan n
mga benepisyo. Ito ib na kailangan ang
atanungan o mag dokumento aho n
oras trabaho. ala baya

Italiano (Italian)

IMPORTANTE! Questo documento contiene informazioni impo n caso cupazione,
respons ità e/o i sussidi. È fondamentale che lei comprenda ni. ande o urre i
ocum ti di diso zione 35-7069 v Le erprete a
olo gr ito.

日本語 (Japanese)

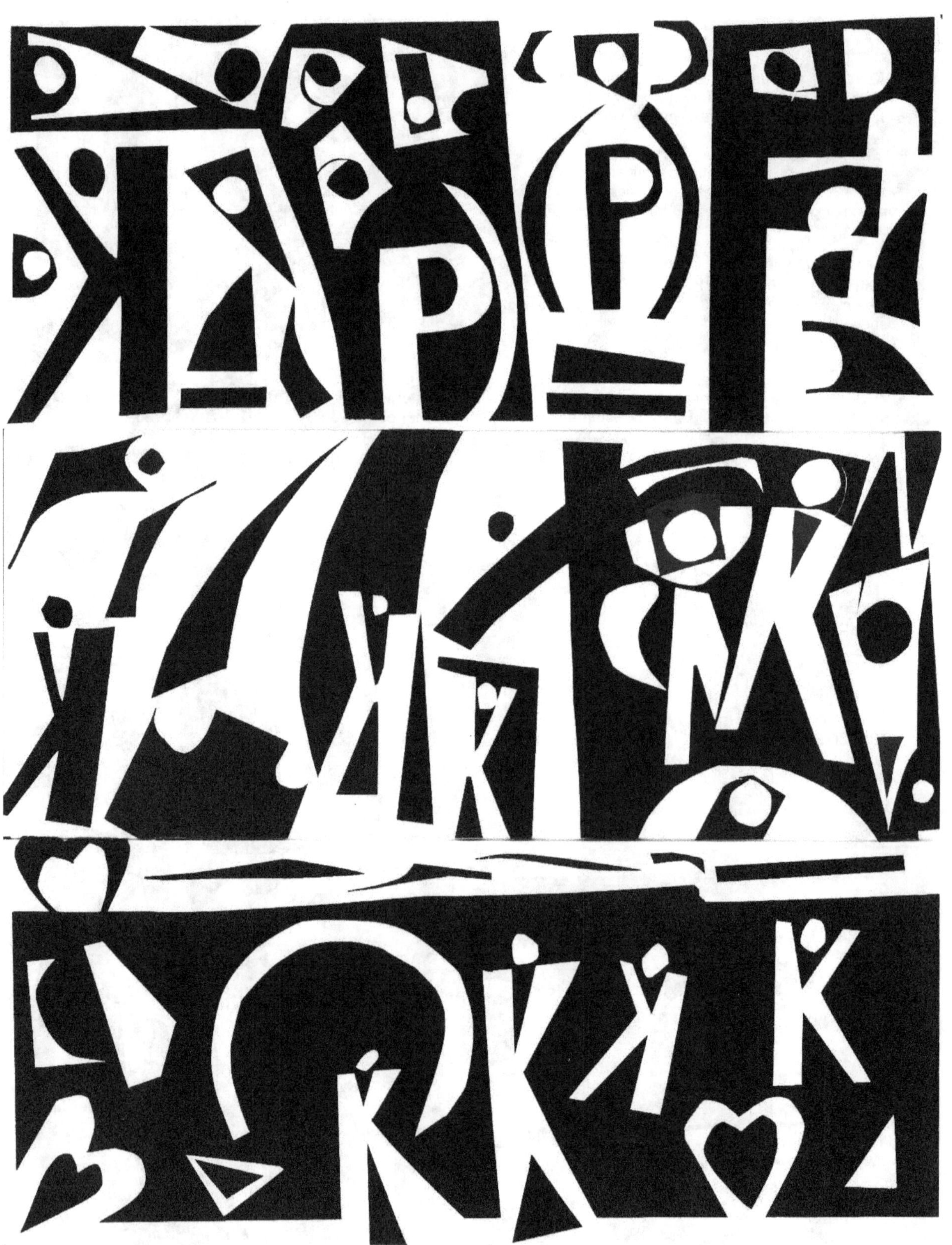

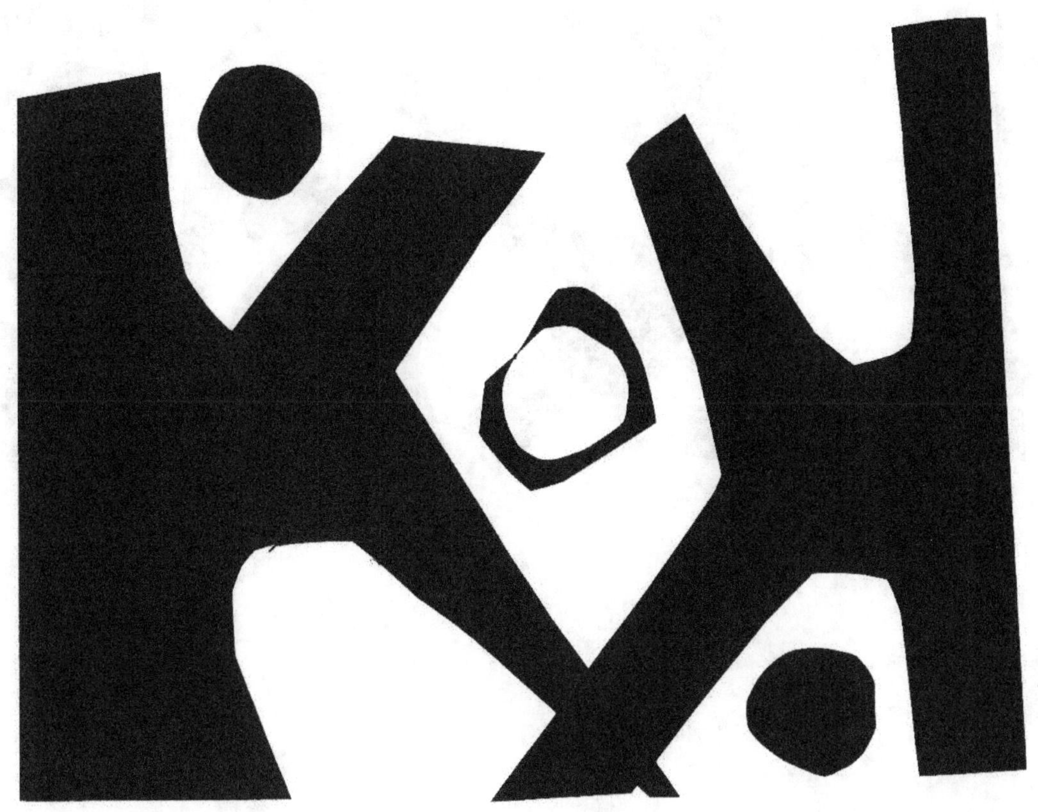

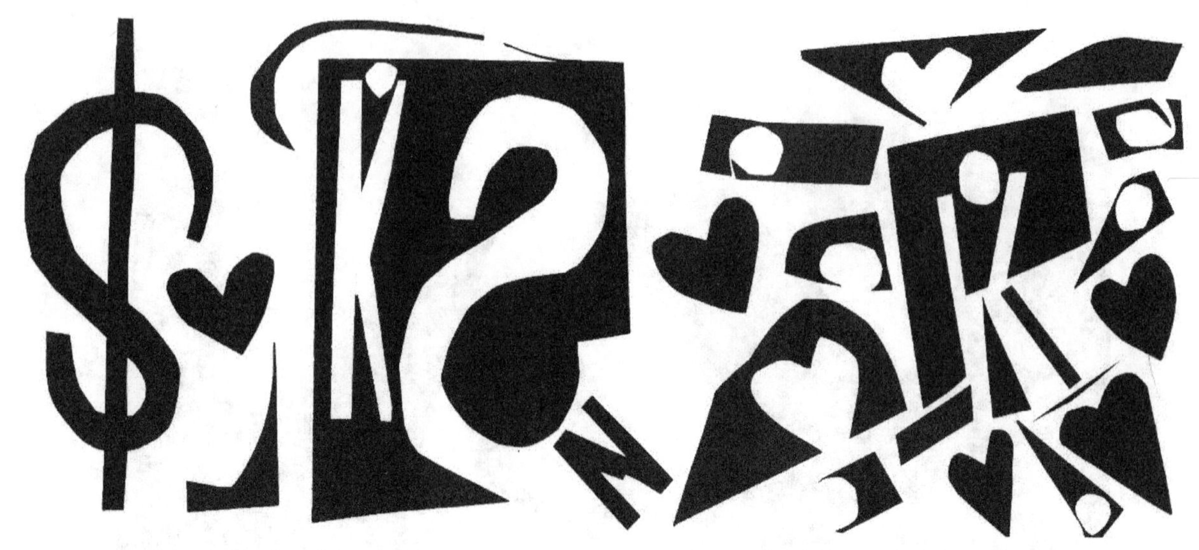

End Notes for *Construction Paper Poems*

Page 1 – *Abstract Glyph*
Page 2 – *W.S.B.* – William Seward Burroughs II - 1900s American Writer, Visual Artist & Spoken Word Performer - original Beat Generation figure, author of *Naked Lunch*, popularized the cut-up method of writing.
Page 4 – *Warhol* – Andy Warhol - 1960s-80s American Pop Artist - collaborated with Jean-Michel Basquiat in the 1980s, the decade of both of their untimely deaths.
Page 6 – This collage uses ephemera via Jon Foster of the mail art network IUOMA.
Page 7 – *T.N.H.* – Thich Nhat Hanh - Vietnamese Buddhist Monk, Poet & Peace Activist - author of more than 100 books in English, including *Teachings on Love*, 1998.
Page 8 – *Jobs* – Steve Jobs - Founder & CEO of Apple Inc. - Walter Isaacson wrote an official biography, *Steve Jobs*, published the year Jobs died of cancer at age 56 in 2011.
Page 9 – *SRV* – Stevie Ray Vaughan - Texan Blues Guitarist circa 1980s
Page 13 – *Snake*
Page 14 – *Death*
Page 18 – *School*
Page 19 – Portrait of a Wisconsin artist who wishes to remain anonymous.
Page 22 – *Pope*
Page 23 – *Patti* – Patti Smith - 1970s Punk Rock Musician, Writer & Poet - published *Just Kids* in 2010, a memoir of her relationship with photographer Robert Mapplethorpe. This glyph was made after seeing the musician in concert at the Barrymore Theatre Sunday August 5th, 2007.
Page 24 – Black Lives Matter (BLM) - Decentralized political and social movement concerning all racially motivated violence against black people, circa 2013. Gained prominence in 2020 after the murder of George Floyd.
Page 30 – *Malcolm* – Malcolm X - Also el-Hajj Malik el-Shabazz, 1960s era American civil rights activist - *The Autobiography of Malcolm X* was published in 1965, the year of his assassination.
Page 31 – *Louie* – Portrait of a coworker at a thrift store attended donation center circa 2005-06
Page 40 – *John* – John Lennon - English singer-songwriter & peace activist circa 1950s-1980s

Page 41 – *Poppy* – Kobayashi Issa - Japanese Haiku Poet known for his love of animal & insect creatures - *Poppy*, a portrait of Issa, is taken from the haiku: Just simply alive/ Both of us, I/ And the poppy.
Page 42 – *Holmes* – Sherlock Holmes - Fictional Private Detective created near the end of the 19th century by British author Sir Arthur Conan Doyle. Actor Jeremy Brett popularized the character in the Granada TV series from 1984 to 1994.
Page 43 – *Fish*
Page 46 – *Ego* – Written/ drawn in hospital the summer of 1998, the 1st sensical concrete poem I created recovering from my initial episode of mania at the age of 24.
Page 47 – *Drink*
Page 49 – *Dog*
Page 51 – *Death*
Page 52 – *Dad* – Leonard William Stolte - Portrait of the author's father
Page 53 – *Crumb* – Robert Crumb - American cartoonist born 1943 - *Crumb* is a 1995 documentary about the artist.
Page 56 – *Cat*
Page 60 – *Bird*
Page 61 – *Le Roi* – Jean-Michel Basquiat - Portrait of the 1980s American Painter - works often employ poetic language similar to works of concrete & visual poetry - themes often related to BLM.
Page 62 – *Baby* – Harper Nicholas Stolte - Portrait of 1st born nephew of the author, 2003

Other books by MT Stolte

Concrete Dollars & Cents Poems
Magnetic Poems
Drilling for Suit Mystery – *with John M. Bennett*

This is eMTeVisPub #13

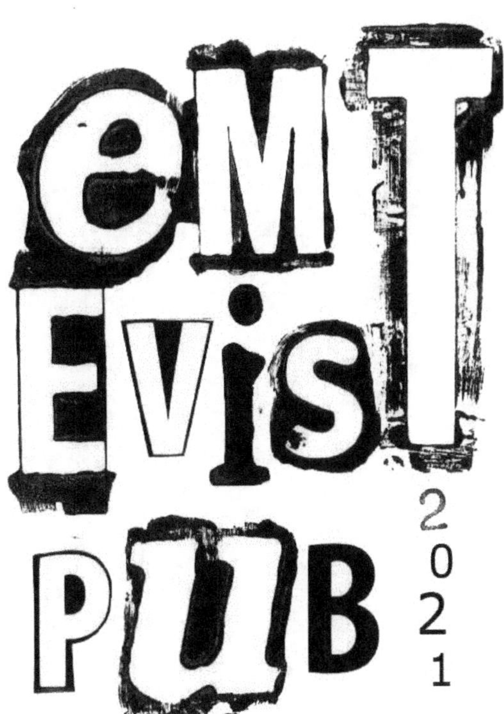

www.ingramcontent.com/pod-product-compliance
Lightning Source LLC
LaVergne TN
LVHW061253100826
845148LV00008B/1116
* 9 7 8 1 7 3 5 3 8 5 0 1 3 *